J. (John) Hannah

The Courtly Poets from Raleigh to Montrose

J. (John) Hannah

The Courtly Poets from Raleigh to Montrose

ISBN/EAN: 9783744693189

Printed in Europe, USA, Canada, Australia, Japan

Cover: Foto ©Thomas Meinert / pixelio.de

More available books at **www.hansebooks.com**

THE COURTLY POETS

FROM RALEIGH TO

MONTROSE

EDITED BY J. HANNAH, D.C.L.

WARDEN OF TRINITY COLLEGE

GLENALMOND

LONDON

BELL AND DALDY YORK STREET

COVENT GARDEN

1870

CHISWICK PRESS:—PRINTED BY WHITTINGHAM AND WILKINS,
TOOKS COURT, CHANCERY LANE.

CONTENTS.

PART I.

THE POEMS OF SIR WALTER RALEIGH NOW FIRST COL-
LECTED AND AUTHENTICATED.

PART II.

CONTENTS.

PART III.

SPECIMENS OF OTHER COURTLY POETS FROM 1540 TO 1650.

x   CONTENTS.

INTRODUCTION.

MY chief design in publishing this small volume is to do an act of justice to the memory of Sir Walter Raleigh, whose poetry has been unaccountably neglected by his biographers, though it is singularly well-fitted to illustrate his character, while it left a distinct mark on the literature of a most brilliant age. No attempt was made during his lifetime, or for long afterwards, to identify or gather up his scattered pieces. The most important of his poems, "Cynthia," has long been lost. The old editions of his "Remains" contain only three short poems. The first responsible editor of his minor writings could only extend the number to nine; and the collection admitted to the standard edition of his works is at once defective and redundant.

It is many years since I called attention to this subject in a volume which was meant, in the first instance, to illustrate the poetry of Sir Henry Wotton and his friends. But as Raleigh's poems formed then a secondary object, my treatment of the question was, in many respects, imperfect; and Raleigh's later biographers and critics, however meritorious on many higher grounds, have continued to repeat the old mistakes, of treating as doubtful some of his best authenticated and most characteristic poems, while quoting as genuine, without a word of warning, the mere waifs and strays of Elizabethan literature, which a zealous collector had swept together under his name.

One is unwilling to let a youthful work remain unfinished, or to feel that any labour has been wasted by being left incomplete. I thought it worth while, therefore, to devote a summer's vacation to the renewal of long-suspended researches among those printed and manuscript miscellanies of the Elizabethan period which are preserved in our great public libraries; and I have thus enabled myself to go over the subject afresh, and more completely, in the present volume, in which Raleigh takes the lead. The authentication of his poetry has been carefully revised and extended; and while I have excluded all the unauthenticated poems from that division of the volume which bears his name, I have been able to include many genuine pieces which had found no previous place among his writings.

I hope it will be thought that the careful sifting to which his poems have been now subjected has caused them to bear a far more distinct witness to the features of his marked yet varied character. At all events it ought to have the effect of giving more point and decisiveness to arguments rested on internal evidence. In this respect, Raleigh's critics have scarcely been fortunate. Mr. Tytler, for instance, thought the lines on Gascoigne's Steel Glass "below his other pieces," and unlikely to have "flowed from the same *sweet vein* which produced the answer to Marlowe's Passionate Shepherd." But surely Raleigh's "vein" was far more frequently sententious than "sweet." Other writers have judged more correctly in accepting the lines as an excellent specimen of his balanced, grave, judicial "censure." "The style is his," says Mr. Kingsley; "solid, stately, epigrammatic." Again, Mr. Hallam said that "The Lie" (called also "The Soul's Errand") had been ascribed to Raleigh "without evidence, and, we may add, without probability." Perhaps the "probability" is more apparent now that conclusive "evidence" has been found. The poem seems to me to be a typical expression of Raleigh's character; his vigour, his scorn, his haughty directness. Assume it to have been written at some moment of disgust and disappointment, and it will be seen to breathe in every line the pride with which he was always ready to confront his adversaries; yet the despondency with which he cried out, even during his first short imprisonment, that now at last his heart was broken; *spes et fortuna valete!* "Do with me now, therefore, what you list. I am more weary of life than they are desirous I should perish." (Edwards, ii. 52; July, 1592.)

As is often the case with men of high courage and really sanguine temperament, Raleigh's thoughts were perpetually saddened by the anticipation of

the end. No small portion of his verses might
have been written, as is actually said of several
pieces, "the night before his death." Dismissing
this tradition, except in the one case where it
seems to be at once strong and probable, we shall
find grounds for supposing that he marked each
crisis of his history by writing some short poem,
in which the vanity of life is proclaimed, under an
aspect suited to his circumstances and age. His
first slight check occurred in 1589, when he went
to visit Spenser in Ireland; and more seriously a
little later, when his secret marriage, or its dis-
creditable preliminaries, sent him to the Tower.
"The Lie," with its proud, indignant brevity,
would then exactly express his angry temper.
"The Pilgrimage" belongs more naturally to a
time when he was smarting under the rudeness of
the king's attorney at his trial in 1603. Viewed
by the light of that unrighteous prosecution, the
grotesque imagery which disturbs its solemn
aspirations may remind us of the more galling of
the annoyances from which he knew that death
would set him free. The few lines, "Even such
is time," mark the calm reality of the now certain
doom; they express the thoughts appropriate for
the night now known to be indeed the last, when
no room remained for bitterness or anger, in the
contemplation of immediate and inevitable death.

The "Continuation of Cynthia" must have
been written very early in his long imprison-
ment, which lasted from December 1603 to March
1616; and again in 1618 from August to October.
The handwriting resembles that of some papers

dated 1603 ; and the fragment could scarcely have
found its way to Hatfield after the death of Robert,
Earl of Salisbury, in 1612.   The internal evidence
points in the same direction.   The whole poem is
coloured by that ruling fiction of the Elizabethan
court, which compelled loyalty to express itself in
the language of a lover-like devotion.   No doubt
Raleigh preserved to his last hour an unshaken
reverence for the memory of his royal mistress.
That stately homage is a leading feature in all his
writings; from the time when he made her the
standard of virtue and beauty (p. 9), in whom
was "virtue's perfect image cast" (p. 78), for
whose "defence we labour all" (p. 6), to the time
when he offered his touching petition to Queen
Anne of Denmark just before his death (p. 53):—

> "That I and mine may never mourn the miss
> Of Her we had, but praise our living Queen."

The author of a well-known epigram caught the
position exactly when he exclaimed, "O hadst
thou served thy Heroine all thy days!"   But it
is not so easy to believe that he could have main-
tained, to any late period of his imprisonment
under James, that conventional form of flattery,
which had continued welcome to the queen to
the last.   The poem contains not the slightest
recognition of those claims on the husband and
the father which must have strengthened their
hold on the heart of the captive, while his loyalty
resumed its more natural and appropriate tenor.
The despondency of his language will not suffice
to prove a later date, because it was his usual tone

under every disappointment. Even as early as
1595-6, at the height of his proud and vigorous
manhood, he could write, in words which remind
us of the very expressions of this fragment: " It
is true that, as my errors were great, so they have
yielded very grievous effects ; and if aught might
have been deserved in former times to have coun-
terpoised any part of [my] offences, *the fruit thereof*
(as it seemeth) was long before *fallen from the tree*,
and the *dead stock* only remained. I did, there-
fore, even *in the winter of my life*, undertake these
travels," &c. (Epistle dedicatory to the Discovery
of Guiana, 1596.) Through a great part of the
piece it might be doubted whether the queen was
really dead, or only dead to him ; *i. e.* whether
the whole were not a mere exaggeration of some
earlier disappointment. Such a notion seems to be
incompatible with the express words of several
passages ; but we cannot suppose that the death
of the queen was long past at the date of his
writing, or the mere lapse of time and change of
circumstance would have forced him to appear in
a larger and nobler character than the conventional
part of a disappointed suitor.

Between fiction and figure, and the obscurity
which hangs over an unfinished work, it is not
easy to carry out any safe biographical interpre-
tation. He begins by saying that his joys " died
when first" his " fancy erred" (p. 32); appa-
rently one of those phrases by which he described
his boldness in seeking another mistress than the
queen. If this is correct, the point of departure
in the poem is not later than 1592. At all events

it is clear that the definite period of "twelve years entire," which he "wasted in this war; twelve years of" his "most happy younger days" (p. 36), must be reckoned from the beginning of his court favour, about 1580, which brings us to the same year, 1592, for its close. From that great check he had now passed, he tells us, into a state of hopelessness, which he describes under a variety of images; amongst which, the complaint that he has now "no feeding flocks, no shepherd's company" (p. 33), reminds us of the days when he talked of Cynthia and her flock with Spenser, under "the green alders by the Mulla's shore." When he tells us that the "memory" of the queen, "more strong than were ten thousand ships of war," had nearly brought him back from his voyage towards "new worlds" in search of gold, and praise, and glory (p. 34), we are reminded that, on his Panama expedition in 1592, she sent after him a more potent summons than her "memory," in the shape of a recall. The images of warmth lingering in the corpse, and heat in winter, and motion in the arrested wheel, are meant to illustrate the tenacity of hope which made him write on, even "in the dust," after his disgrace; and the reality mingles with the figure when he speaks, in almost the very language of the preface to his History, of the cheerless work of beginning, by the fading light of life's evening, "to write the story of all ages past" (p. 36). The distraction which he describes on p. 37 could be paralleled from his correspondence. "The tokens hung on breast and kindly worn" (p. 41), may

b

refer to the interchange of toys between the queen and her courtiers; as when she sent to Sir H. Gilbert "a token from her Majesty, an anchor guided by a lady," with a request for his picture in return. A "ring with a diamond which he weareth on his finger, given him by the late Queen," was among the jewels found on Raleigh's person after his execution. It would be possible, but precarious, to trace a reference in other passages to the loss of Sherborne, and to the disappointed expectations which had so often attracted him towards the western world. His closing words are simple and touching (p. 50):—

> " Thus home I draw, as death's long night draws on;
>   Yet every foot, old thoughts turn back mine eyes:
> Constraint me guides, as old age draws a stone
>   Against the hill, which over-weighty lies
>
> For feeble arms or wasted strength to move:
>   My steps are backward, gazing on my loss,
> My mind's affection and my soul's sole love,
>   Not mixed with fancy's chaff or fortune's dross.
>
> To God I leave it, who first gave it me,
>   And I her gave, and she returned again,
> As it was hers; so let His mercies be
>   Of my last comforts the essential mean.
>
> But be it so or not, the effects are past;
>   Her love hath end; my woe must ever last."

With the poems of Raleigh and Wotton I have now combined what may be accepted, I hope, as a fairly representative collection of the minor poetry of those "courtly makers," who kept up the succession to Surrey and Wyatt through the eventful century, which intervened between the death of Henry VIII. and the execution of Charles I. They are strictly the Courtly Poets of England, though the line ends with a famous Scottish name, which forms the more appropriate conclusion to the series, because it is known that Raleigh's History of the World was one of the favourite studies which moulded the boyhood of Montrose.

There are scarcely half-a-dozen pieces in this volume which we owe to poets by profession. Most of these poems are little more than the comparatively idle words of busy men, whose end " was not writing, even while they wrote ;" those occasional sayings in which the character often reveals itself more clearly than in studied language. There is a special charm in compositions which have amused the leisure of distinguished persons, who have won their spurs in very different fields ; of statesmen, soldiers, students and divines. who have used metre as the mere outlet for transitory feelings, to give grace to a compliment, or terseness to the expression of a sudden emotion. or point and beauty to a calm reflection. To a great extent, such poems are likely to be imitative ; and in that aspect they form a curiously exact measure of the influence exerted by a style or fashion. But several of the pieces which are brought together here may claim a higher rank than this. Raleigh himself was a man of marked original power, which has left its record in his poems, as well as in his larger works, and in the varied achievements of his chequered life. He wrote a sonnet which Milton did not disdain to imitate. The Archbishop of Dublin says that " there have been seldom profounder thoughts more perfectly expressed " than in part of his

" Poesy to prove Affection is not Love." His poem called " The Lie " is probably the best instance of a poetical outburst of anger and scorn, which we can find throughout the minor literature of the proud and hasty Tudor times. His " Pilgrimage," with all its quaintness, is perhaps the most striking example of so-called death-bed verses. His reply to Marlowe remains even yet unrivalled, as the retort of polished common-sense to the conventionalities of pastoral poetry. Even when tested by this higher standard, the other courtiers whose verses are here represented are not unworthy to take their places by the side of Raleigh. But their poetry will also render us the minor service of enabling us to trace the changes in the tone of English society from one critical period to another ; through intervals of gloom under Mary, and boundless energy under Elizabeth, and suspense under James, till the light-hearted gaiety of older England revived amidst the waning fortunes of Charles's cavaliers. By the side of much formal adulation, we can trace a vein of that manly self-respect, which has always formed the mainstay of our public life ; and a strong under-current of that religious feeling, which the darkest days could never hide. And we can also trace a deepening range of thought, and a richer harmony of verse, and a growing smoothness and facility of language, which bear witness to the influence of those greater writers, who sustain the main weight of the reputation of the Elizabethan age.

J. H.

Trinity College, Glenalmond,
January 28, 1870.

APPENDIX A.

EARLY EXTRACTS ON RALEIGH'S POETRY AND LIFE.

I. THE CRITICS.

1.

OR ditty and amorous ode, I find Sir Walter Raleigh's vein most lofty, insolent, and passionate."— Puttenham's "Art of English Poesy," 1589, p. 51.

2. Francis Meres mentions Sir Walter Raleigh as one of "the most passionate among us to bewail and bemoan the perplexities of love."—"Palladis Tamia," 1598, p. 154, repr.

3. Edmund Bolton speaks of his prose works, "Guiana, and his prefatory epistle before his mighty undertaking in the History of the World," as "full of proper, clear, and courtly graces of speech;" and couples his English poems with those of Donne, Holland, and Lord Brooke as "not easily to be mended."—"Hypercritica," *circ.* 1610, pp. 249, 251, repr.

4. Gabriel Harvey is said, in some MS. notes on Chaucer, to have called Raleigh's "Cynthia" "a fine and sweet invention."—Malone's "Shakespeare," by Boswell, ii. 579.

5. "He who writeth the Art of English Poesy praiseth much Raleigh and Dyer; but their works are so few that are come to my hands, I cannot well say anything of them."—Drummond of Hawthornden, "Works," 1711, p. 226.

6. "Sir Walter Raleigh, a person both sufficiently known in history, and by his 'History of the World,' seems also by the character given him by the author of the 'Art of English Poetry' [Puttenham, as above], to have expressed

himself more a poet than the little we have extant of his
poetry seems to import."—Edward Phillips, " Theatrum
Poetarum," 1675, ii. 233.

EDMUND SPENSER.

1. " Considering she beareth two persons, the one of a
most royal Queen or Empress, the other of a most virtuous
and beautiful Lady, this latter part in some places I do ex-
press in Belphœbe, fashioning her name according to your
own excellent conceit of Cynthia,—Phœbe and Cynthia being
both names of Diana."—Letter of the Author's (of the " Faery
Queen") to Sir Walter Raleigh, 1590; Spenser's " Works,"
by Collier, i. 149.

2.

" To thee, that art the summer's nightingale,
  Thy sovereign Goddess's most dear delight,
Why do I send this rustic madrigal,
  That may thy tuneful ear unseason quite?
  Thou only fit this argument to write,
In whose high thoughts pleasure hath built her bower,
  And dainty love learned sweetly to indite.
My rhymes I know unsavoury and sour,
To taste the streams that, like a golden shower,
  Flow from thy fruitful head, of thy love's praise;
Fitter, perhaps, to thunder martial stower,
  When so thee list thy lofty Muse to raise:
Yet, till that thou thy poem wilt make known,
Let thy fair Cynthia's praises be thus rudely shewn."

(Sonnet to Sir Walter Raleigh, printed with the first three
    books of the " Faery Queen," in 1590; *ib.* i. 164.)

3.

" But if in living colours and right hue
  Thyself thou covet to see pictured,
Who can it do more lively or more true
  Than that sweet verse, with nectar sprinkled,
  In which a gracious servant pictured
His Cynthia, his heaven's fairest light?
  That with his melting sweetness ravished,
And with the wonder of her beams bright,
My senses lulled are in slumber of delight.

" But let that same delicious poet lend
  A little leave unto a rustic Muse

To sing his mistress' praise; and let him mend,
  If ought amiss her liking may abuse:
Ne let his fairest Cynthia refuse
In mirrors more than one herself to see;
  But either Gloriana let her choose,
Or in Belphœbe fashioned to be;
In th' one her rule, in th' other her rare chastity."

(Introduction to the third book of the
"Faery Queen," ib. ii. 336.)

4.

" ' One day,' quoth he, 'I sat, as was my trade,
  Under the foot of Mole, that mountain hoar,
Keeping my sheep amongst the coolly shade
  Of the green alders by the Mulla's shore:
There a strange shepherd chanced to find me out,
  Whether allured with my pipe's delight, ·
Whose pleasing sound ysbrilled far about,
  Or thither led by chance, I know not right:
Whom when I asked from what place he came,
  And how he hight, himself he did ycleepe
The Shepherd of the Oceän by name,
  And said he came far from the main-sea deep.
He, sitting me beside in that same shade,
  Provoked me to play some pleasant fit;
And, when he heard the music which I made,
  He found himself full greatly pleased at it:
Yet, æmuling my pipe, he took in hond
  My pipe, before that æmuled of many,
And played thereon, for well that skill he conned,
  Himself as skilful in that art as any.
He piped, I sung; and, when he sung, I piped;
  By change of turns each making other merry;
Neither envying other, nor envied,
  So piped we, until we both were weary."

* * * * *

" His song was all a lamentable lay
  Of great unkindness and of usage hard,
Of Cynthia, the Lady of the Sea,
  Which from her presence faultless him debarred.
And ever and anon, with singulfs rife,
  He cried out, to make his undersong,
' Ah, my love's Queen, and Goddess of my life!
  Who shall me pity, when thou dost me wrong?' "

* * * * *

"And there that Shepherd of the Ocean is,
    That spends his wit in love's consuming smart;
Full sweetly tempered is that Muse of his,
    That can empierce a prince's mighty heart."

("Colin Clout's come home again," 1591; *ib.* v. 33, 37, 47.)

III. SPECIMENS OF LAMPOONS ON RALEIGH.

1.

" *Water* thy plants with grace divine,
    And hope to live for aye;
Then to thy Saviour Christ incline;
    In Him make steadfast stay;
Raw is the reason that doth *lie*
    Within an atheist's head,
Which saith the soul of man doth die,
    When that the body's dead.

"Now may you see the sudden fall
    Of him that thought to climb full high;—
A man well known unto you all,
    Whose state, you see, doth stand *Rawly.*"
                                        &c. &c. &c.

(The first eight lines printed in four as *Raleigh's own
composition*, in the Oxford edition of his works, viii. 732,
with the title "Moral Advice." They were taken from
MS. Ashm. 781, p. 163, where they are signed "Sr. Wa.
Raleigh." Also printed with a continuation, of which the
above specimen will be sufficient, among Mr. Halliwell's
"Poetical Miscellanies" from MSS.; Percy Society, vol. xv.
p. 14. The Oxford editors failed to observe the pun on
Raleigh's name, to which James I. also condescended on a
famous occasion.)

2.

"Watt, I wot well thy overweening wit,
    Led by ambitious humours, wrought thy fall,"
                                        &c. &c. &c.

"I pity that the *summer's nightingale,*[1]
    Immortal Cynthia's sometime dear delight,
That used to sing so sweet a madrigal,
    Should like an owl go wanderer in the night,

---

[1] Quoted from Spenser's "Sonnet," above, p. xxii. The
phrase was also adopted by Drayton; see Collier's "Bibl.
Cat." i. 224-5; and note on Spenser.

Hated of all, but pitied of none,
Though swanlike now he makes his dying moan."

(Extracted from a long piece in Mr. Halliwell's "Poetical Miscellanies," as above, pp. 15, 16. The last line is important, as proving that Raleigh was believed to have written verses shortly before his death.)

3.

"The Nightingale will scarce be tame,
    No company keep he can;
He dare not show his face for shame;
    He feareth the look of man:
But Robin like a man can look,
    And doth shun no place;
He will sing in every nook,
    And stare you in the face."

(Extracted from a piece published from Gough's MSS. in the "Camden Society's Miscellany," iii. 22; and interpreted of the quarrel between Raleigh and Essex in Collier's "Life of Spenser," p. lxix.)

4.

"To whom shall cursed I my case complain,
    To move some pity of my wretched state?
For though no other comfort doth remain
    Yet pity would my grief extenuate:
For I towards God and man myself abused,
And therefore am of God and man refused.

"To Heaven I dare not lift my wretched eyes,
    Nor ask for pardon for my wretched deeds;
For I His word and service did despise,
    Esteeming them of no more worth than weeds:
[From] which most vile conceits these woes proceeds;
For now I find, and, finding, fear to rue,
There is a God who is both just and true," &c.

(From "The despairing Complaint of wretched Raleigh for his treacheries wrought against the worthy Essex;" MS. Ashm. 36, p. 11. The piece contains forty-one stanzas, each of seven lines except the first.)

5.

"I speak to such, if any such there be,
    Who are possessed, through their Prince's grace,

With swelling pride and scornful insolency,
   Haughty disdaining and abuse or place:
To such I say, if any such there be,
   Come, see these vices punished in me!" &c.

(From " Raleigh's Caveat to secure Courtiers;" following
the above in the same MS.; thirty-eight stanzas of six lines
each.)

IV.

ANSWERS TO " THE LIE;" CHIEFLY SUCH AS CONNECT
RALEIGH WITH THAT POEM.

1.

Go, echo of the mind, a careless truth protest;
Make answer that *rude Rawly* no stomach can digest:
For why ? *The lie's* descent is over base to tell;
To us it came from Italy; to them it came from hell.
What reason proves, confess; what slander saith, deny:
Let no untruth with triumph pass; but never give the lie!
Confess, in glittering court all are not gold that shine;
Yet say one pearl and much fine gold g[l]ows in the prince's
      mind.
Confess that many [weeds] do overgrow the ground;
Yet say, within the field of God good corn is to be found.
Confess, some judge unjust the widow's right delay;
Yet say there are some Samuels that never say her nay.
Admit, some man of state do pitch his thoughts too high;
Is that a rule for all the rest, their loyal hearts to try?
Your wits are in the wane; your autumn in the bud;
You argue from particulars; your reason is not good.
And still that men may see less reason to commend you,
I marvel most, amongst the rest, how schools and arts offend
      you.
But why pursue I thus the witless words of wind?
The more the crab doth seek to creep, the more she is behind.
In church and commonwealth, in court and country both,
What! nothing good? but all [s]o bad that every man doth
      loathe?
The further that you range, your error is the wider;
The bee sometimes doth honey suck, but sure you are a
      spider!
And so my counsel is, for that you want a name,
To seek some corner in the dark to hide yourself from shame.
There wrap the silly fly within your spiteful web;

Both church and court may want you well; they are not at
  such ebb.
As quarrels once begun are not so quickly ended,
So many faults may soon be found, but not so soon amended.
  And when you come again to give the world the lie,
I pray you tell them how to live, and teach them how to die.

(Chetham MS. 8012, p. 107, each line as two. First
printed by me, partially in 1842, and at length in 1845.)

2. *The Answer to the Lie.*

Court's scorn, state's disgracing, potentates' scoff, govern-
  ments' defacing,
Princes' touch, church's unhallowing, arts' injury, virtue's
  debasing,
Age's monster, honour's wasting, beauty's blemish, favour's
  blasting,
Wit's excrement, wisdom's vomit, physic's scorn, law's comet,
Fortune's child, valour's defiler, justice' revenger, friendship's
  beguiler,
Such is the song, such is the author; worthy to be rewarded
  with a halter.

Erroris Responsio.

Court's commender, state's maintainer, potentate's defender,
  governments' gainer,
Princes' praiser, church's preacher, arts' raiser, virtue's
  teacher,
Age's rewarder, honour's strengthener, beauty's guarder,
  favour's lengthener,
Wit's admirer, wisdom's scholar, physic's desirer, law's fol-
  lower,
Fortune's blamer, nature's observer, justice' proclaimer,
  friendship's preserver;
Such is the author, such is the song; returning the halter,
  contemning the wrong.   Sr. Wa. Ra.

(MS. Ashm. 781, p. 164. Printed from that MS. *among
Raleigh's own poems* in the Oxford edition of his works, viii.
735.)

3. *Extract from another Contemporary*
Answer to the Lie.

St. 2.

" The Court hath settled sureness
  In banishing such boldness;

The Church retains her pureness,
   Though Atheists show their coldness:
The Court and Church, though base,
   Turn lies into thy face."

St. 3.

" The Potentates reply,
   Thou base, by them advanced,
Sinisterly soarest high,
   And at their actions glanced:
They, for this thankless part,
   Turn lies into thy heart," &c.

(MS. Tann. 306, fol. 188; written stanza by stanza at the side of a copy of the original poem.)

V.

The Reaction after his Death.

1.

" O hadst thou served thy Heroine all thy days!
Had Heaven from storms of envy screened thy bays!
Hadst thou still flourished in a warlike reign,
Thy sword had made a conquest, like thy pen!
But nought to such untimely fate could bring
The *valiant subject*, but a *coward king*."

(" Phœnix Britannicus," 1732, p. 453; Oldys' " Life of Raleigh," p. clxxxv., slightly altered. I have taken one word from Oldys' copy.)

2.

" I will not weep; for 'twere as great a sin
To shed a tear for thee, as to have been
An actor in thy death. Thy life and age
Was but a various scene on Fortune's stage,
With whom thou tugg'st and strov'st even out of breath
In thy long toil, ne'er mastered till thy death;
And then, despite of trains and cruel wit,
Thou didst at once subdue malice and it.

" I dare not then so blast thy memory
As say I do lament or pity thee.
Were I to choose a subject to bestow
My pity on, he should be one as low
In spirit as desert; that durst not die,
But rather were content by slavery
To purchase life: or I would pity those,

Thy most industrious and friendly foes,
Who, when they thought to make thee scandal's story,
Lent thee a swifter flight to heaven and glory;
That thought, by cutting off some withered days
Which thou could'st spare them, to eclipse thy praise;
Yet gave it brighter foil; made thy ag'd fame
Appear more white and fair than foul their shame;
And did promote an execution
Which, but for them, nature and age had done.

"Such worthless things as these were only born
To live on pity's alms, too mean for scorn.
Thou diedst an envious wonder, whose high fate
The world must still admire, scarce imitate."

(From Bishop Henry King's "Poems, Elegies, Paradoxes,
and Sonnets," 1657, p. 97, as "An Elegy upon S. W. R."
Also in Oldys, p. ccxxxi.)

3.

"Great heart, who taught thee thus to die,
Death yielding thee the victory?
Where took'st thou leave of life? If here,
How could'st thou be so free from fear?
But sure thou diedst, and quittedst the state
Of flesh and blood before that fate:
Else what a miracle were wrought,—
To triumph both in life and thought!
I saw in every stander by
Pale Death; Life only in thine eye.
The legacy thou gav'st, we then
Will sue for, when thou diest again.
Farewell! Truth shall this story say,—
We died,—thou only livedst that day!"

(Printed in Shirley's "Life of Raleigh," *ad fin.*, as "a
taste of the poetry of those times." It occurs in MS. Rawl.
Misc. 699, p. 35, along with the preceding elegy; also
among the Hawthornden MSS. vol. viii. as by "A. B.," and
was printed from this last copy by Mr. Laing, "Arch.
Scot." iv. 238.)

APPENDIX B.

ALPHABETICAL LIST OF POEMS WHICH HAVE BEEN ASCRIBED TO SIR W. RALEIGH WITHOUT OR AGAINST EVIDENCE.

1.

"ARE women fair? aye, wondrous fair to see too."— Included among "Poems supposed to be written by Sir W. Raleigh," in the Lee Priory ed. of Davison's " Poetical Rhapsody," vol. ii. p. 89, on no evidence but the signature "Ignoto." Title, " An Invective against Women." An anonymous copy in the Percy folio; see Furnivall's edit. vol. iii. p. 364.

2. " As at noon Dulcina rested."—Given to Raleigh in Ellis's " Specimens," edit. 1801 (not retained in edit. 1811). Thence Cayley and Brydges, and the Oxford editors. No evidence whatever. An anonymous copy in the Percy folio; see Furnivall's edit. vol. iv. p. 82.

3. " Come, gentle herdman, sit by me."—Among Raleigh's poems in Lee Priory ed. of Davison's " Poetical Rhapsody" (as above), vol. ii. p. 92. No evidence but the signature " Ignoto." Title, " Eclogue."

4. " Come, live with me and be my dear."—E. H., p. 216, as a second reply to Marlowe's song (see this vol. p. 10). It is headed, " Another of the same nature made since," and signed " Ignoto." Hence claimed for Raleigh by Ellis, Cayley, Brydges, and the Oxford editors.

5. " Corydon, arise, my Corydon."—E. H., p. 73, signed " Ignoto." Hence claimed for Raleigh by Brydges and the Oxford editors. There is an anonymous copy in the " Crown-Garland of Golden Roses," 1612, p. 63, repr.

6. " Court's commender, state's maintainer."—A defence of " The Lie " in the Ashm. MSS.; claimed for Raleigh by the Oxford editors. (See it in this vol. above, p. xxvii.)

7. " Court's scorn, state's disgracing."—The attack to which the above is a reply. Printed among Raleigh's poems by the Oxford editors. (See it in this vol. above, p. xxvii.)

8 " Eternal mover, whose diffused glory."—Sir Henry Wotton's (see it in this vol. p. 91). Erroneously claimed for Raleigh in the " Topographer," on the authority of a B. M. MS.

9. " Farewell, ye gilded follies, pleasing troubles!"— Author uncertain. (See it in this vol. p. 109.) Ascribed to Raleigh by Sir H. Nicolas, without any known authority.

10. " Hey, down-a-down, did Dian sing."—E. H., p. 135, as " A Nymph's disdain of Love," signed " Ignoto." Hence claimed for Raleigh by Brydges and the Oxford editors.

11. " If love be life, I long to die."—E. H., p. 211, as " Dispraise of love and lovers' follies," signed " Ignoto." Hence claimed for Raleigh by Brydges and the Oxford editors. It was added in the second ed. of E. H., from Davison's " Poetical Rhapsody," and is really by A. W.

12. " In Peascod time, when hound to horn."—E. H., p. 206, as " The Shepherd's Slumber," signed " Ignoto" in the first edition. Hence claimed for Raleigh by Brydges and the Oxford editors.

13. " It chanced of late a shepherd's swain."—In the first part of the Lee Priory ed. of Davison's " Poetical Rhapsody," vol. i. p. 17, as " a Fiction how Cupid made a Nymph wound herself with his arrows." Brydges " suspected" it " to be Raleigh's, as well from internal evidence, as because it had the signature of ' Anomos' (!) in the edition of 1602." Ibid. p. 40; see also his Introduction, p. 39, and " Exc. Tudor." ii. 123. It has been ascribed to Sidney Godolphin, though written, as Percy remarks, " before he was born." It is really by A. W.

14. " Lady, my flame still burning."—The first part of a " Dialogue betwixt the Lover and his Lady" (see No. 23). Included among Raleigh's supposed poems in the Lee Priory ed. of Davison's " Poetical Rhapsody " (as before), vol. ii. p. 88. No evidence but the signature " Ignoto."

15. " Like desert woods with darksome shades obscured." —E. H., p. 224, as " Thyrsis the shepherd to his pipe," signed " Ignoto." Hence claimed for Raleigh by Brydges and the Oxford editors. It is either by Lodge or Dyer (see note in this vol. p. 245).

16. " Love is the link, the knot, the band of unity."—Included among Raleigh's supposed poems in the Lee Priory

ed. of Davison's " Poetical Rhapsody," vol. ii. p. 90. No evidence but the signature " Ignoto."

17. " Man's life's a tragedy : his mother's womb."— Marked " Ignoto " in " Rel. Wotton." and hence claimed for Raleigh by Brydges and the Oxford editors; (see it in this vol. p. 120.)

18. " My prime of youth is but a frost of cares."—Tych-bourne's verses; (see them in this vol. p. 114.) Mr. D'Israeli says that "they have at one time been assigned to Raleigh ;" on what authority I do not know.

19. " My wanton Muse, that whilome wont to sing."— E. H., p. 225, as " An heroical poem," signed " Ignoto." Hence claimed for Raleigh by Ellis, Cayley, Brydges, and the Oxford editors; (see it in this vol. p. 179.) It was added to the second ed. of E. H., from Davison's " Poetical Rhapsody," and is really by A. W.

20. " Now have I learnt with much ado at last."—E. H., p. 241, as " a Defiance to disdainful Love," signed " Ignoto." Hence claimed for Raleigh by Ellis, Cayley, Brydges, and the Oxford editors. It was added to the second ed. of E. H., from Davison's " Poetical Rhapsody," and is really by A. W.

21. " Quivering fears, heart-tearing cares."—Marked " Ignoto " in " Rel. Wotton." and hence claimed for Raleigh by Brydges and the Oxford editors; (see it in this volume, p. 106.)

22. " Rise, O my soul! with thy desires to heaven."— Marked " Ignoto" in " Rel. Wotton." and hence claimed for Raleigh by Brydges and the Oxford editors; (see it in this vol. p. 116.)

23. " Sweet Lord, your flame still burning."—The lady's answer to the piece here numbered 14. Included among Raleigh's supposed Poems in the Lee Priory ed. of Davison's " Poetical Rhapsody," vol. ii. p. 88. No evidence but the signature " Ignoto."

24. " Sweet violets, Love's Paradise, that spread."— E. H., p. 161, as " The shepherd to the flowers," signed " Ignoto." Hence claimed for Raleigh by Ellis, Cayley, Brydges, and the Oxford editors; (see it in this vol. p. 174.)

25. " The fairest pearls that northern seas do breed."—

E. H., p. 236, as " Love the only price of love," signed
" Ignoto." Hence claimed for Raleigh by Brydges and the
Oxford editors   It was added to the second ed. of E. H.,
from Davison's " Poetical Rhapsody," and is really by
A. W.

26. " The frozen snake oppressed with heaped snow."—
E. H., p. 230, as " The lover's absence kills me, her pre-
sence kills [*al.* cures] me," signed " Ignoto." Hence claimed
for Raleigh by Brydges and the Oxford editors.   It was
added to the second ed. of E. H., from Davison's " Poetical
Rhapsody," and is really by A. W.

27. " Water thy plants with grace divine," &c.—An at-
tack on Raleigh, inserted among his Poems from the Ashm.
MSS. by the Oxford editors; (see it in this vol. above, p.
xxiv.)

28. " Whilst my soul's eye beheld no light."—Marked
" Ignoto" in " Rel. Wotton." and hence claimed for Raleigh
by Brydges, but *not* by the Oxford editors; (see it in this
vol. p. 111.)

PART I.

THE POEMS OF

SIR WALTER RALEIGH

NOW FIRST COLLECTED AND

AUTHENTICATED.

B

THE POEMS OF
SIR WALTER RALEIGH.

I.

WALTER RAWELY OF THE MIDDLE TEMPLE

IN COMMENDATION OF THE STEEL GLASS.[1]
(1576.)

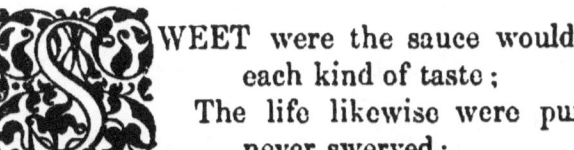WEET were the sauce would please
  each kind of taste;
  The life likewise were pure that
  never swerved:
For spiteful tongues in cankered stomachs placed
 Deem worst of things which best (percase)
  deserved.
But what for that? This medicine may suffice
To scorn the rest, and seek to please the wise.

Though sundry minds in sundry sort do deem,
 Yet worthiest wights yield praise for every pain;

[1] Prefixed to George Gascoigne's "Steel Glass," 1576.

But envious brains do nought, or light, esteem
  Such stately steps as they cannot attain:
For whoso reaps renown above the rest,
With heaps of hate shall surely be oppressed.

Wherefore, to write my censure of this book,
  This Glass of Steel unpartially doth show
Abuses all to such as in it look,
  From prince to poor, from high estate to low.
As for the verse, who list like trade to try,
I fear me much, shall hardly reach so high.

II.

THE EXCUSE.

WRITTEN BY SIR WALTER RALEIGH IN HIS YOUNGER YEARS.[1]

CALLING to mind, my *eyes* went long
      about
        To cause my heart for to forsake my
          breast,
All in a rage I sought to pull them out,
  As who had been such traitors to my rest:

[1] Oldys' "Life of Raleigh," p. lv., "from the copy of a celebrated lady, Lady Isabella Thynne, who probably had it out of the family." Quoted by Puttenham in 1589, as "a most excellent ditty, written by Sir Walter Raleigh." In MS. Ashm. 781, p. 138, it has the signature "Sr. Wa: Raleigh;" and in "Wit's Interpreter," 1671, p. 205, it is described as "by Sir Walter Raleigh." In the "Phœnix Nest," 1593, p. 72, in MS. Harl. 6910, fol. 142, *verso,* and in MS. Rawl. 85, fol. 104, *verso,* it is anonymous.

What could they say to win again my grace?—
Forsooth, that they had seen my mistress' face.

Another time, my *heart* I called to mind,—
   Thinking that he this woe on me had brought,
Because that he to love his force resigned,
   When of such wars my fancy never thought:
What could he say when I would him have slain?—
That he was hers, and had forgone my chain.

At last, when I perceived both eyes and heart
   Excuse themselves, as guiltless of my ill,
I found *myself* the cause of all my smart,
   And told myself that I myself would kill:
Yet when I saw myself to you was true,
I loved myself, because myself loved you.

III.

AN EPITAPH

UPON THE RIGHT HONOURABLE SIR PHILIP SIDNEY,

KNIGHT, LORD GOVERNOR OF FLUSHING.[1]

(Died Oct. 7, 1586.)

O praise thy life or wail thy worthy death,
   And want thy wit,—thy wit high,
      pure, divine,—
   Is far beyond the power of mortal line,
Nor any one hath worth that draweth breath;

[1] Quoted in 1591, by Sir J. Harington, as Sir W. Raleigh's; also at a later date by Drummond of Hawthornden. Printed anonymously in the "Phœnix Nest," 1593, p. 8, and with Spenser's "Astrophel," 1595, Sign. K 2.

Yet rich in zeal (though poor in learning's lore),
 And friendly care obscured in secret breast,
 And love that envy in thy life suppressed,—
Thy dear life done,—and death hath doubled more.

And I, that in thy time and living state
 Did only praise thy virtues in my thought,
 As one that seeld the rising sun hath sought,
With words and tears now wail thy timeless fate.

Drawn was thy race aright from princely line;
 Nor less than such, by gifts that nature gave,—
 The common mother that all creatures have,—
Doth virtue show, and princely lineage shine.

A king gave thee thy name; a kingly mind,—
 That God thee gave,—who found it now too dear
 For this base world, and hath resumed it near
To sit in skies, and sort with powers divine.

Kent thy birth-days, and Oxford held thy youth;
 The heavens made haste, and stayed nor years
   nor time;
 The fruits of age grew ripe in thy first prime;
Thy will, thy words; thy words the seals of truth.

Great gifts and wisdom rare employed thee thence,
 To treat from kings with those more great than
   kings;
 Such hope men had to lay the highest things
On thy wise youth, to be transported hence.

Whence to sharp wars sweet honour did thee call,
 Thy country's love, religion, and thy friends;
 Of worthy men the marks, the lives, and ends,
And her defence, for whom we labour all.

There didst thou vanquish shame and tedious age,
  Grief, sorrow, sickness, and base fortune's might;
  Thy rising day saw never woeful night,
But passed with praise from off this worldly stage.

Back to the camp by thee that day was brought,
  First thine own death; and after, thy long fame;
  Tears to the soldiers; the proud Castilian's shame;
Virtue expressed, and honour truly taught.

What hath he lost that such great grace hath won?
  Young years for endless years, and hope unsure
  Of fortune's gifts for wealth that still shall dure:
O happy race, with so great praises run!

England doth hold thy limbs, that bred the same;
  Flanders thy valour, where it last was tried;
  The camp thy sorrow, where thy body died;
Thy friends thy want; the world thy virtue's fame;

Nations thy wit; our minds lay up thy love;
  Letters thy learning; thy loss years long to come;
  In worthy hearts sorrow hath made thy tomb;
Thy soul and spright enrich the heavens above.

Thy liberal heart embalmed in grateful tears,
  Young sighs, sweet sighs, sage sighs, bewail thy
    fall;
  Envy her sting, and spite hath left her gall;
Malice herself a mourning garment wears.

That day their Hannibal died, our Scipio fell,—
  Scipio, Cicero, and Petrarch of our time;
  Whose virtues, wounded by my worthless rhyme,
Let angels speak, and heaven thy praises tell.

IV.

A VISION UPON THIS CONCEIT OF THE FAIRY QUEEN.[1]

(1590.)

ETHOUGHT I saw the grave where
    Laura lay,
    Within that temple where the vestal
      flame
Was wont to burn : and, passing by that way,
  To see that buried dust of living fame,
Whose tomb fair Love and fairer Virtue kept,
  All suddenly I saw the Fairy Queen,
At whose approach the soul of Petrarch wept ;
  And from thenceforth those graces were not seen,
For they this Queen attended ; in whose stead
  Oblivion laid him down on Laura's hearse.
Hereat the hardest stones were seen to bleed,
  And groans of buried ghosts the heavens did
      pierce :
Where Homer's spright did tremble all for grief,
And cursed the access of that celestial thief.

[1] Appended to Spenser's " Fairy Queen," books i.-iii.,
1590, p. 596.

V.

ANOTHER OF THE SAME.[1]

(1590.)

THE praise of meaner wits this work like
 profit brings,
  As doth the cuckoo's song delight when
   Philumena sings.
If thou hast formed right true virtue's face herein,
Virtue herself can best discern, to whom they
  written bin.
If thou hast beauty praised, let her sole looks
  divine
Judge if aught therein be amiss, and mend it by
  her eine.
If Chastity want aught, or Temperance her due,
Behold her princely mind aright, and write thy
  Queen anew.
Meanwhile she shall perceive how far her virtues
  soar
Above the reach of all that live, or such as wrote
  of yore:
And thereby will excuse and favour thy good will,
Whose virtue cannot be expressed but by an angel's
  quill.
Of me no lines are loved nor letters are of price,
Of all which speak our English tongue, but those
  of thy device.

[1] From the same; signed W. R.

VI.

REPLY TO MARLOWE.

1. MARLOWE'S SONG.

THE PASSIONATE SHEPHERD TO HIS LOVE.[1]

(Before 1593.)

COME live with me, and be my love ;
And we will all the pleasures prove
That hills and valleys, dales and fields,
Woods, or steepy mountain yields.

And we will sit upon the rocks,
Seeing the shepherds feed their flocks
By shallow rivers, to whose falls
Melodious birds sing madrigals.

And I will make thee beds of roses,
And a thousand fragrant posies ;
A cap of flowers, and a kirtle
Embroidered all with leaves of myrtle ;

A gown made of the finest wool
Which from our pretty lambs we pull ;
Fair-lined slippers for the cold,
With buckles of the purest gold ;

[1] Dyce's " Marlowe," iii. 299. An imperfect copy was
printed in the " Passionate Pilgrim " in 1599, and it is
quoted in the " Merry Wives of Windsor," iii. 1.   It was
printed at length with Marlowe's name in " England's
Helicon," 1600 ; and also in Walton's "Complete Angler,"
1653, as " that smooth song which was made by Kit Mar-
low, now at least fifty years ago."   Marlowe died *sixty*
years before,—in 1593.

A belt of straw and ivy-buds,
With coral clasps and amber-studs:
And if these pleasures may thee move,
Come love with me, and be my love.

The shepherd-swains shall dance and sing
For thy delight each May-morning;
If these delights thy mind may move,
Then live with me, and be my love.

2. RALEIGH'S REPLY.

(Before 1599.)

IF all the world and love were young,
And truth in every shepherd's tongue,
These pretty pleasures might me move
To live with thee and be thy love.

But time drives flocks from field to fold,
When rivers rage and rocks grow cold;
And Philomel becometh dumb;
The rest complains of cares to come.

The flowers do fade, and wanton fields
To wayward winter reckoning yields:
A honey tongue, a heart of gall,
Is fancy's spring, but sorrow's fall.

---

[1] The first verse was printed in the " Passionate Pilgrim "
in 1599, and the whole in " England's Helicon," 1600, where
the signature is *Ignoto.*   Also in Walton's "Complete
Angler," 1653, as " made by Sir Walter Raleigh in his
younger days."

Thy gowns, thy shoes, thy beds of roses,
Thy cap, thy kirtle, and thy posies,
Soon break, soon wither, soon forgotten,—
In folly ripe, in reason rotten.

Thy belt of straw and ivy buds,
Thy coral clasps and amber studs,—
All those in me no means can move
To come to thee and be thy love.

But could youth last, and love still breed ;
Had joys no date, nor age no need ;
Then those delights my mind might move
To live with thee and be thy love.

VII.

LIKE HERMIT POOR.[1]

(Before 1593.)

LIKE hermit poor in pensive place obscure
        I mean to spend my days of endless
            doubt,
    To wail such woes as time cannot recure,
Where nought but love shall ever find me out.
And at my gates despair shall linger still,
To let in death when love and fortune will.

[1] Ascribed to Raleigh in "To-day a Man, to-morrow none," 1643-4; King's Pamphlets, B. M. vol. 139. It is anonymous in the "Phœnix Nest," 1593, p. 69; in "Tixall Poetry," p. 115; in MS. Rawl. 85, fol. 21, *verso*; in Harl. MS. 6910, fol. 139, *verso*, &c.

A gown of grief my body shall attire,
   And broken hope shall be my strength and stay;
And late repentance, linked with long desire,
   Shall be the couch whereon my limbs I'll lay.
And at my gates despair shall linger still,
To let in death when love and fortune will.

My food shall be of care and sorrow made;
   My drink nought else but tears fallen from mine
      eyes;
And for my light, in such obscured shade,
   The flames may serve which from my heart arise.
And at my gates despair shall linger still,   .
To let in death when love and fortune will.

VIII.

FAREWELL TO THE COURT.[1]

(Before 1593.)

IKE truthless dreams, so are my joys
        expired,
     And past return are all my dandled
        days,
My love misled, and fancy quite retired;
   Of all which past, the sorrow only stays.

[1] Signed W. R., with the above title, in "Le Prince
d'Amour," 1660, p. 132, and on that authority, acknow-
ledged by Oldys, p. clxxiii. note, and inserted in the Oxford
edition of Raleigh's "Works," viii. 730: correctly, for it is
quoted as his own by Raleigh himself in the Hatfield MS.;
see No. XX. line 144. There is an anonymous copy in the
"Phœnix Nest," 1593, p. 70.

My lost delights, now clean from sight of land,
  Have left me all alone in unknown ways,
My mind to woe, my life in fortune's hand;
  Of all which past, the sorrow only stays.

As in a country strange without companion,
  I only wail the wrong of death's delays,
Whose sweet spring spent, whose summer well nigh
        done ;
  Of all which past, the sorrow only stays ;

Whom care forewarns, ere age and winter cold,
To haste me hence to find my fortune's fold.

IX.

THE ADVICE.[1]

MANY desire, but few or none deserve
        To win the fort of thy most constant
        will ;
      Therefore take heed ; let fancy never
      swerve
But unto him that will defend thee still :
For this be sure, the fort of fame once won,
Farewell the rest, thy happy days are done !

Many desire, but few or none deserve
  To pluck the flowers, and let the leaves to fall ;

---

[1] Signed W. R., like the last piece, in "Le Prince d'Amour,"
1660, p. 133 ; and therefore accepted by Oldys and the Ox-
ford editors, viii. 731.   There is an anonymous copy in
MS. Rawl. Poet. 85, fol. 116, as " written to Mrs A. V."

Therefore take heed ; let fancy never swerve
  But unto him that will take leaves and all :
For this be sure, the flower once plucked away,
Farewell the rest, thy happy days decay !

Many desire, but few or none deserve
  To cut the corn, not subject to the sickle ;
Therefore take heed ; let fancy never swerve,
  But constant stand, for mowers' minds are fickle ;
For this be sure, the crop being once obtained,
Farewell the rest, the soil will be disdained.

X.

IN THE GRACE OF WIT, OF TONGUE, AND FACE.[1]

(Before 1593.)

ER face, her tongue, her wit, so fair, so
      sweet, so sharp,
  First bent, then drew, now hit, mine
      eye, mine ear, my heart :
Mine eye, mine ear, my heart, to like, to learn, to love,

[1] A shorter copy than the above occurs anonymously in the "Phœnix Nest," 1593, p. 71, and is repeated in "Le Prince d'Amour," 1660, p. 131, as "The Lover's Maze," with the signature W. R., as in the last two cases. Hence it was accepted by Oldys and the Oxford editors, viii. 730. The above copy is taken from Davison's " Poetical Rhapsody," where it is anonymous; the title from editions 1611 and 1621. In editions 1602 and 1608, it is called " A reporting Sonnet."

Her face, her tongue, her wit, doth lead, doth teach,
    doth move:
Her face, her tongue, her wit, with beams, with
    sound, with art,
Doth blind, doth charm, doth rule, mine eye, mine
    ear, my heart.

Mine eye, mine ear, my heart, with life, with hope,
    with skill,
Her face, her tongue, her wit, doth feed, doth feast,
    doth fill:
O face, O tongue, O wit, with frowns, with checks,
    with smart,
Wring not, vex not, wound not, mine eye, mine ear,
    my heart:
This eye, this ear, this heart, shall joy, shall bind,
    shall swear
Your face, your tongue, your wit, to serve, to love,
    to fear.

XI.

FAIN WOULD I, BUT I DARE NOT.[1]

FAIN would I, but I dare not; I dare,
    and yet I may not;
I may, although I care not, for pleasure
    when I play not.

[1] MS. Rawl. 85, fol. 41, *verso*, with the signature " W. R."
in apparently a later hand: thence inserted in the Oxford
edition of Raleigh's " Works," vol. viii. p. 732, with the
title " A Lover's Verses." There is an anonymous copy of
the first three stanzas in Harl. MS. 6910, fol. 154.

You laugh because you like not; I jest whenas I
    joy not;
You pierce, although you strike not; I strike and
    yet annoy not.

I spy, whenas I speak not; for oft I speak and
    speed not;
But of my wounds you reck not, because you see
    they bleed not:
Yet bleed they where you see not, but you the pain
    endure not:
Of noble mind they be not that ever kill and cure
    not.

I see, whenas I view not; I wish, although I
    crave not;
I serve, and yet I sue not; I hope for that I
    have not;
I catch, although I hold not; I burn, although I
    flame not;
I seem, whenas I would not; and when I seem, I
    am not.

Yours am I, though I seem not, and will be, though
    I show not;
Mine outward deeds then deem not, when mine
    intent you know not;
But if my serving prove not most sure, although I
    sue not,
Withdraw your mind and love not, nor of my ruin
    rue not.

XII.

SIR WALTER RALEIGH TO HIS SON.[1]

THREE things there be that prosper all
    apace,
    And flourish while they are asunder
    far;
But on a day, they meet all in a place,
  And when they meet, they one another mar.

And they be these; the Wood, the Weed, the Wag:
  The Wood is that that makes the gallows tree;
The Weed is that that strings the hangman's bag;
  The Wag, my pretty knave, betokens thee.

Now mark, dear boy—while these assemble not,
  Green springs the tree, hemp grows, the wag
    is wild;
But when they meet, it makes the timber rot,
  It frets the halter, and it chokes the child.

GOD BLESS THE CHILD!

[1] MS. Malone 19, p. 130.

XIII.

ON THE CARDS AND DICE.[1]

BEFORE the sixth day of the next new
        year,
        Strange wonders in this kingdom shall
        appear :
Four kings shall be assembled in this isle,
Where they shall keep great tumult for awhile.
Many men then shall have an end of crosses,
And many likewise shall sustain great losses ;
Many that now full joyful are and glad,
Shall at that time be sorrowful and sad ;
Full many a Christian's heart shall quake for fear,
The dreadful sound of *trump* when he shall hear.
Dead bones shall then be tumbled up and down,
In every city and in every town.
By day or night this tumult shall not cease,
Until an herald shall proclaim a peace ;
An herald strong, the like was never born,
Whose very beard is flesh and mouth is horn.

S^r WAL. R.

---

[1] MS. Malone 19, p. 45. Also ascribed to Raleigh in the
Catalogue of Oxford MSS. among those of C. C. C.

XIV.

THE SILENT LOVER.[1]

ASSIONS are likened best to floods and
          streams :
      The shallow murmur, but the deep
      are dumb ;
So, when affections yield discourse, it seems
   The bottom is but shallow whence they come.
They that are rich in words, in words discover
That they are poor in that which makes a lover.

Wrong not, sweet empress of my heart,
   The merit of true passion,
With thinking that he feels no smart,
   That sues for no compassion ;

Since, if my plaints serve not to approve
   The conquest of thy beauty,
It comes not from defect of love,
   But from excess of duty.

[1] Signed as below in a MS. formerly belonging to the
late Mr. Pickering. The text of the Oxford edition, viii. 716,
is corrected from a Rawl. MS. where the piece is absurdly
headed " Sir Walter Raleigh to Queen Elizabeth." Also
assigned to Raleigh in the Lansdowne MS. of some of W.
Browne's Poems (Brydges, Preface to Browne's Poems, L. P.
1815, p. 6). In other old copies entitled " To his Mistress. by
Sir Walter Raleigh ;" see " Wit's Interpreter," 1671, p. 146 ;
another copy on p. 173 is anonymous. The title given above
is from Oldys, p. lv. and the editions of Raleigh's Works.
The piece has been claimed on inferior evidence for Lord
Pembroke, Sir R. Aytoun, and Lord Walden.

For, knowing that I sue to serve
   A saint of such perfection,
As all desire, but none deserve,
   A place in her affection,

I rather choose to want relief
   Than venture the revealing;
Where glory recommends the grief,
   Despair distrusts the healing.

Thus those desires that aim too high
   For any mortal lover,
When reason cannot make them die,
   Discretion doth them cover.

Yet, when discretion doth bereave
   The plaints that they should utter,
Then thy discretion may perceive
   That silence is a suitor.

Silence in love bewrays more woe
   Than words, though ne'er so witty:
A beggar that is dumb, you know,
   May challenge double pity.

Then wrong not, dearest to my heart,
   My true, though secret, passion:
He smarteth most that hides his smart,
   And sues for no compassion.

                    Sʳ W. R.

XV.

A POESY TO PROVE AFFECTION
IS NOT LOVE.[1]

(Before 1602.)

ONCEIT, begotten by the eyes,
Is quickly born and quickly dies;
For while it seeks our hearts to have,
Meanwhile, there reason makes his
     grave;
For many things the eyes approve,
Which yet the heart doth seldom love.

For as the seeds in spring time sown
Die in the ground ere they be grown,
Such is conceit, whose rooting fails,
As child that in the cradle quails;
Or else within the mother's womb
Hath his beginning and his tomb.

Affection follows Fortune's wheels,
And soon is shaken from her heels;
For, following beauty or estate,
Her liking still is turned to hate;
For all affections have their change,
And fancy only loves to range.

Desire himself runs out of breath,
And, getting, doth but gain his death:

[1] Davison's " Poetical Rhapsody," 1602-1621.

Desire nor reason hath nor rest,
And, blind, doth seldom choose the best:
Desire attained is not desire,
But as the cinders of the fire.

As ships in ports desired are drowned,
As fruit, once ripe, then falls to ground,
As flies that seek for flames are brought
To cinders by the flames they sought;
So fond desire when it attains,
The life expires, the woe remains.

And yet some poets fain would prove
Affection to be perfect love;
And that desire is of that kind,
No less a passion of the mind;
As if wild beasts and men did seek
To like, to love, to choose alike.

W. R.

XVI.

THE LIE.[1]

(Certainly before 1608; possibly before 1596.)

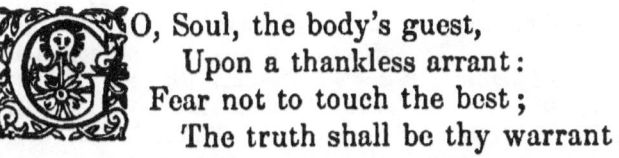O, Soul, the body's guest,
   Upon a thankless arrant:
Fear not to touch the best;
   The truth shall be thy warrant:

[1] Signed "Wa: Raleigh" in MS. Chetham, 8012, p. 103,
and headed "Sir Walter Wrawly his lye" in a MS. of Mr.
Collier's; see his "Bibl. Cat.," vol. ii. p. 224. Also ascribed

Go, since I needs must die,
And give the world the lie.

Say to the court, it glows
    And shines like rotten wood ;
Say to the church, it shows
    What's good, and doth no good :
If church and court reply,
Then give them both the lie.

Tell potentates, they live
    Acting by others' action ;
Not loved unless they give,
    Not strong but by a faction :
If potentates reply,
Give potentates the lie.

Tell men of high condition,
    That manage the estate,
Their purpose is ambition,
    Their practice only hate :
And if they once reply,
Then give them all the lie.

to Raleigh by name in a contemporary answer in the Chetham
MS. p. 107, and by implication in some other early replies ;
see appendix to the Introduction, A. No. IV.   It was in-
serted by Birch in 1751 among Raleigh's " Minor Works,"
vol. ii. p. 396, as " The Farewell." Many other old copies are
anonymous; e. g. in Davison's " Poetical Rhapsody," 1608-
1621 (p. 100); in MS. Tann., 306, fol. 188; in Harl. MS.
6910, fol. 141, verso, and in Harl. MS. 2296, fol. 135. Some
of these texts contain both additions and mutilations; and
spurious copies are found among the poems of Sylvester,
p. 652, editions 1633 and 1641, and of Lord Pembroke,
p. 104, edition 1660.

Tell them that brave it most,
   They beg for more by spending,
Who, in their greatest cost,
   Seek nothing but commending:
And if they make reply,
Then give them all the lie.

Tell zeal it wants devotion;
   Tell love it is but lust;
Tell time it is but motion;
   Tell flesh it is but dust:
And wish them not reply,
For thou must give the lie.

Tell age it daily wasteth;
   Tell honour how it alters;
Tell beauty how she blasteth;
   Tell favour how it falters:
And as they shall reply,
Give every one the lie.

Tell wit how much it wrangles
   In tickle points of niceness;
Tell wisdom she entangles
   Herself in over-wiseness:
And when they do reply,
Straight give them both the lie.

Tell physic of her boldness;
   Tell skill it is pretension;
Tell charity of coldness;
   Tell law it is contention:
And as they do reply,
So give them still the lie.

Tell fortune of her blindness;
 Tell nature of decay;
Tell friendship of unkindness;
 Tell justice of delay:
And if they will reply,
Then give them all the lie.

Tell arts they have no soundness,
 But vary by esteeming;
Tell schools they want profoundness,
 And stand too much on seeming:
If arts and schools reply,
Give arts and schools the lie.

Tell faith it's fled the city;
 Tell how the country erreth;
Tell manhood shakes off pity;
 Tell virtue least preferreth:
And if they do reply,
Spare not to give the lie.

So when thou hast, as I
 Commanded thee, done blabbing,—
Although to give the lie
 Deserves no less than stabbing,—
Stab at thee he that will,
No stab the soul can kill.

XVII.

SIR WALTER RALEIGH'S PILGRIMAGE.[1]

(*Circ.* 1603?)

GIVE me my scallop-shell of quiet,
        My staff of faith to walk upon,
    My scrip of joy, immortal diet,
        My bottle of salvation,
My gown of glory, hope's true gage;
And thus I'll take my pilgrimage.

Blood must be my body's balmer;
    No other balm will there be given;
Whilst my soul, like quiet palmer,
    Travelleth towards the land of heaven;
Over the silver mountains,
Where spring the nectar fountains:
        There will I kiss
        The bowl of bliss;
And drink mine everlasting fill
Upon every milken hill.
My soul will be a-dry before;
But after, it will thirst no more.

[1] In MS. Ashm. 38, No. 70, it is entitled " Verses made
by Sr. Walter Raleigh the night before he was beheaded;"
a date probably taken by inference from the closing lines.
In a MS. belonging to the late Mr. Pickering, the title is
the same as is here given from the old editions of Raleigh's
" Remains." There are many other early copies; in the
best of which the two concluding lines are omitted.

Then by that happy blissful day,
  More peaceful pilgrims I shall see,
That have cast off their rags of clay,
  And walk apparelled fresh like me.
      I'll take them first
      To quench their thirst
    And taste of nectar suckets,
      At those clear wells
      Where sweetness dwells,
    Drawn up by saints in crystal buckets.

And when our bottles and all we
Are filled with immortality,
Then the blessed paths we'll travel,
Strowed with rubies thick as gravel;
Ceilings of diamonds, sapphire floors,
High walls of coral and pearly bowers.
From thence to heaven's bribeless hall,
Where no corrupted voices brawl;
No conscience molten into gold,
No forged accuser bought or sold,
No cause deferred, no vain-spent journey,
For there Christ is the king's Attorney,
Who pleads for all without degrees,
And He hath angels, but no fees.
And when the grand twelve-million jury
Of our sins, with direful fury,
Against our souls black verdicts give,
Christ pleads His death, and then we live.

Be Thou my speaker, taintless pleader,
Unblotted lawyer, true proceeder!
Thou givest salvation even for alms;
Not with a bribed lawyer's palms.

And this is mine eternal plea
To Him that made heaven, earth, and sea,
That, since my flesh must die so soon,
And want a head to dine next noon,
Just at the stroke, when my veins start and spread,
Set on my soul an everlasting head!
Then am I ready, like a palmer fit,
To tread those blest paths which before I writ.

Of death and judgment, heaven and hell,
Who oft doth think, must needs die well.

XVIII.[1]

HAT is our life? The play of passion.
Our mirth? The music of division:
Our mothers' wombs the tiring-houses
be,
Where we are dressed for life's short comedy.
The earth the stage; Heaven the spectator is,
Who sits and views whosoe'er doth act amiss.
The graves which hide us from the scorching sun
Are like drawn curtains when the play is done.
Thus playing post we to our latest rest,
And then we die in earnest, not in jest.

Sr W. R.

[1] From a MS. formerly belonging to the late Mr. Pickering. It was printed anonymously in a music-book of 1612; see "Censura Lit.," vol. ii. p. 103, 2nd edition; and is found also in MS. Ashm. 36, p. 35, and MS. Ashm. 38, fol. 154.

XIX.

TO THE TRANSLATOR OF LUCAN.[1]

(1614.)

HAD Lucan hid the truth to please the time,
    He had been too unworthy of thy pen,
    Who never sought nor ever cared to climb
    By flattery, or seeking worthless men.
For this thou hast been bruised; but yet those scars
  Do beautify no less than those wounds do,
Received in just and in religious wars;
    Though thou hast bled by both, and bearest
      them too.
Change not! To change thy fortune 'tis too late:
  Who with a manly faith resolves to die,
May promise to himself a lasting state, ·
  Though not so great, yet free from infamy.
Such was thy Lucan, whom so to translate,
Nature thy muse like Lucan's did create.

                  W. R.

[1] Prefixed to Sir A. Gorges' translation of Lucan's
" Pharsalia," 1614.

XX.

CONTINUATION OF THE LOST POEM, CYNTHIA;

NOW FIRST PUBLISHED FROM THE HATFIELD MSS.[1]

(1604-1618?)

I.

F Cynthia be a Queen, a princess, and
    supreme,
    Keep these among the rest, or say it was
      a dream ;
For those that like, expound, and those that loathe,
    express
Meanings according as their minds are moved more
    or less.
For writing what thou art, or showing what thou
    were,
Adds to the one disdain, to the other but despair.
    Thy mind of neither needs, in both seeing it
      exceeds.

II.

    My body in the walls captived
Feels not the wounds of spiteful envy ;
    But my thralled mind, of liberty deprived,
Fast fettered in her ancient memory,
    Doth nought behold but sorrow's dying face :
Such prison erst was so delightful,
    As it desired no other dwelling place :
But time's effects and destinies despiteful

Hatfield MSS., vol. cxliv., fol. 238, *sqq.* "In Sir
Walter's own hand."

Have changed both my keeper and my fare.
Love's fire and beauty's light I then had store;
But now, close kept, as captives wonted are,
That food, that heat, that light, I find no more.
Despair bolts up my doors; and I alone
Speak to dead walls; but those hear not my moan.

III.

THE 21st AND LAST BOOK OF THE OCEAN, TO CYNTHIA.

UFFICETH it to you, my joys interred,
  In simple words that I my woes
    complain:
  You that then died when first my fancy
    erred,—
Joys under dust that never live again?

If to the living were my muse addressed,
  Or did my mind her own spirit still inhold,
Were not my living passion so repressed
  As to the dead the dead did these unfold,

Some sweeter words, some more becoming verse
  Should witness my mishap in higher kind;
But my love's wounds, my fancy in the hearse,
  The idea but resting of a wasted mind,

The blossoms fallen, the sap gone from the tree.
  The broken monuments of my great desires.—
From these so lost what may the affections be?
  What heat in cinders of extinguished fires?

Lost in the mud of those high-flowing streams,
   Which through more fairer fields their courses
      bend,
Slain with self-thoughts, amazed in fearful dreams,
   Woes without date, discomforts without end:

From fruit[less] trees I gather withered leaves,
   And glean the broken ears with miser's hand,
Who sometime did enjoy the weighty sheaves;
   I seek fair flowers amid the brinish sand.

All in the shade, even in the fair sun days,
   Under those healthless trees I sit alone,
Where joyful birds sing neither lovely lays,
   Nor Philomen recounts her direful moan.

No feeding flocks, no shepherd's company,
   That might renew my dolorous conceit,
While happy then, while love and fantasy
   Confined my thoughts on that fair flock to wait;

No pleasing streams fast to the ocean wending,
   The messengers sometimes of my great woe;
But all on earth, as from the cold storms bending,
   Shrink from my thoughts in high heavens or below.

Oh, hopeful love, my object and invention,
   Oh, true desire, the spur of my conceit,
Oh, worthiest spirit, my mind's impulsion,
   Oh, eyes transpersant, my affection's bait;

Oh, princely form, my fancy's adamant,
   Divine conceit, my pains' acceptance,
Oh. all in one! oh, heaven on earth transparent!
   The seat of joys and love's abundance!

D

Out of that mass of miracles, my muse
    Gathered those flowers, to her pure senses
        pleasing;
Out of her eyes, the store of joys, did choose
    Equal delights, my sorrow's counterpoising.

Her regal looks my vigorous sighs suppressed;
    Small drops of joys sweetened great worlds of
        woes;
One gladsome day a thousand cares redressed;—
    Whom love defends, what fortune overthrows?

When she did well, what did there else amiss?
    When she did ill, what empires would have
        pleased?
No other power effecting woe or bliss,
    She gave, she took, she wounded, she appeased.

The honour of her love love still devising,
    Wounding my mind with contrary conceit,
Transferred itself sometime to her aspiring,
    Sometime the trumpet of her thought's retreat.

To seek new worlds for gold, for praise, for glory,
    To try desire, to try love severed far,
When I was gone, she sent her memory,
    More strong than were ten thousand ships of war:

To call me back, to leave great honour's thought,
    To leave my friends, my fortune, my attempt;
To leave the purpose I so long had sought,
    And hold both cares and comforts in contempt.

Such heat in ice, such fire in frost remained,
    Such trust in doubt, such comfort in despair,
Which, like the gentle lamb, though lately weaned,
    Plays with the dug, though finds no comfort there.

But as a body, violently slain,
  Retaineth warmth although the spirit be gone,
And by a power in nature moves again
  Till it be laid below the fatal stone;

Or as the earth, even in cold winter days,
  Left for a time by her life-giving sun,
Doth by the power remaining of his rays
  Produce some green, though not as it hath done;

Or as a wheel, forced by the falling stream,
  Although the course be turned some other way,
Doth for a time go round upon the beam,
  Till, wanting strength to move, it stands at stay;

So my forsaken heart, my withered mind,—
  Widow of all the joys it once possessed,
My hopes clean out of sight with forced wind,
  To kingdoms strange, to lands far-off addressed,

Alone, forsaken, friendless, on the shore
  With many wounds, with death's cold pangs
    embraced,
Writes in the dust, as one that could no more,
  Whom love, and time, and fortune, had defaced;

Of things so great, so long, so manifold,
  With means so weak, the soul even then depicting
The weal, the woe, the passages of old,
  And worlds of thoughts described by one last
    sighing.

As if, when after Phœbus is descended,
  And leaves a light much like the past day's
    dawning,
And, every toil and labour wholly ended,
  Each living creature draweth to his resting,

We should begin by such a parting light
  To write the story of all ages past,
And end the same before the approaching night.

Such is again the labour of my mind,
  Whose shroud, by sorrow woven now to end,
Hath seen that ever shining sun declined,
  So many years that so could not descend,

But that the eyes of my mind held her beams
  In every part transferred by love's swift thought;
Far off or near, in waking or in dreams,
  Imagination strong their lustre brought.

Such force her angelic appearance had
  To master distance, time, or cruelty;
Such art to grieve, and after to make glad;
  Such fear in love, such love in majesty.

My weary lines her memory embalmed;
  My darkest ways her eyes make clear as day.
What storms so great but Cynthia's beams appeased?
  What rage so fierce, that love could not allay?

Twelve years entire I wasted in this war;
  Twelve years of my most happy younger days;
But I in them, and they now wasted are:
  " Of all which past, the sorrow only stays."

So wrote I once, and my mishap foretold,
  My mind still feeling sorrowful success;
Even as before a storm the marble cold
  Doth by moist tears tempestuous times express,

So felt my heavy mind my harms at hand,
  Which my vain thought in vain sought to recure:
At middle day my sun seemed under land,
  When any little cloud did it obscure.

And as the icicles in a winter's day,
   Whenas the sun shines with unwonted warm,
     *   *   *

So did my joys melt into secret tears ;
   So did my heart dissolve in wasting drops :
And as the season of the year outwears,
   And heaps of snow from off the mountain tops

With sudden streams the valleys overflow,
   So did the time draw on my more despair :
Then floods of sorrow and whole seas of woe
   The banks of all my hope did overbear,

And drowned my mind in depths of misery :
   Sometime I died ; sometime I was distract,
My soul the stage of fancy's tragedy ;
   Then furious madness, where true reason lacked,

Wrote what it would, and scourged mine own
     conceit.
   Oh, heavy heart ! who can thee witness bear ?
What tongue, what pen, could thy tormenting treat,
   But thine own mourning thoughts which present
     were ?

What stranger mind believe the meanest part ?
   What altered sense conceive the weakest woe,
That tare, that rent, that pierced thy sad heart ?

And as a man distract, with triple might
   Bound in strong chains doth strive and rage in
     vain,
Till, tired and breathless, he is forced to rest,—
   Finds by contention but increase of pain,
And fiery heat inflamed in swollen breast ;

So did my mind in change of passion
    From woe to wrath, from wrath return to woe,
Struggling in vain from love's subjection;

Therefore, all lifeless and all helpless bound,
    My fainting spirits sunk, and heart appalled.
My joys and hopes lay bleeding on the ground,
    That not long since the highest heaven scaled.

I hated life and cursed destiny;
    The thoughts of passed times, like flames of hell,
Kindled afresh within my memory
    The many dear achievements that befell

In those prime years and infancy of love,
    Which to describe were but to die in writing;
Ah, those I sought, but vainly, to remove,
    And vainly shall, by which I perish living.

And though strong reason hold before mine eyes
    The images and forms of worlds past,
Teaching the cause why all those flames that rise
    From forms external can no longer last,

Than that those seeming beauties hold in prime
    Love's ground, his essence, and his empery,
All slaves to age, and vassals unto time,
    Of which repentance writes the tragedy:—

But this my heart's desire could not conceive,
    Whose love outflew the fastest flying time,
A beauty that can easily deceive
    The arrest of years, and creeping age outclimb.

A spring of beauties which time ripeth not—
    Time that but works on frail mortality;
A sweetness which woe's wrongs outwipeth not.
    Whom love hath chose for his divinity;

A vestal fire that burns but never wasteth,
    That loseth nought by giving light to all,
That endless shines each where, and endless lasteth,
    Blossoms of pride that can nor fade nor fall;

These were those marvellous perfections,
    The parents of my sorrow and my envy,
Most deathful and most violent infections;
    These be the tyrants that in fetters tie

Their wounded vassals, yet nor kill nor cure,
    But glory in their lasting misery—
That, as her beauties would, our woes should dure—
    These be the effects of powerful empery.

Yet have these wounders want, which want com-
    . passion;
    Yet hath her mind some marks of human race;
Yet will she be a woman for a fashion,
    So doth she please her virtues to deface.

And like as that immortal power doth seat
    An element of waters, to allay
The fiery sunbeams that on earth do beat,
    And temper by cold night the heat of day,

So hath perfection, which begat her mind,
    Added thereto a change of fantasy,
And left her the affections of her kind,
    Yet free from every evil but cruelty.

But leave her praise; speak thou of nought but
    woe;
Write on the tale that sorrow bids thee tell;
Strive to forget, and care no more to know
    Thy cares are known, by knowing those too well.

Describe her now as she appears to thee;
    Not as she did appear in days fordone:
In love, those things that were no more may be,
    For fancy seldom ends where it begun.

And as a stream by strong hand bounded in
    From nature's course where it did sometime run,
By some small rent or loose part doth begin
    To find escape, till it a way hath won;

Doth then all unawares in sunder tear
    The forced bounds, and, raging, run at large
In the ancient channels as they wonted were;
    Such is of women's love the careful charge,—

Held and maintained with multitude of woes;
    Of long erections such the sudden fall:
One hour diverts, one instant overthrows,
    For which our lives, for which our fortune's thrall

So many years those joys have dearly bought;
    Of which when our fond hopes do most assure,
All is dissolved; our labours come to nought;
    Nor any mark thereof there doth endure:

No more than when small drops of rain do fall
    Upon the parched ground by heat updried;
No cooling moisture is perceived at all,
    Nor any show or sign of wet doth bide.

But as the fields, clothed with leaves and flowers,
    The banks of roses smelling precious sweet,
Have but their beauty's date and timely hours,
    And then, defaced by winter's cold and sleet,
      *   *   *   *   *
So far as neither fruit nor form of flower
    Stays for a witness what such branches bare,
But as time gave, time did again devour,
    And change our rising joy to falling care:

So of affection which our youth presented;
    When she that from the sun reaves power and
        light,
Did but decline her beams as discontented,
    Converting sweetest days to saddest night,

All droops, all dies, all trodden under dust,
    The person, place, and passages forgotten;
The hardest steel eaten with softest rust,
    The firm and solid tree both rent and rotten.

Those thoughts, so full of pleasure and content,
    That in our absence were affection's food,
Are razed out and from the fancy rent;
    In highest grace and heart's dear care that stood,

Are cast for prey to hatred and to scorn,—
    Our dearest treasures and our heart's true joys;
The tokens hung on breast and kindly worn,
    Are now elsewhere disposed or held for toys.

And those which then our jealousy removed,
    And others for our sakes then valued dear,
The one forgot, the rest are dear beloved,
    When all of ours doth strange or vild appear.

Those streams seem standing puddles, which before
 We saw our beauties in, so were they clear;
Belphœbe's course is now observed no more;

That fair resemblance weareth out of date;
 Our ocean seas are but tempestuous waves,
And all things base, that blessed were of late . . . . .

And as a field, wherein the stubble stands
 Of harvest past, the ploughman's eye offends;
He tills again, or tears them up with hands,
 And throws to fire as foiled and fruitless ends,

And takes delight another seed to sow;
 So doth the mind root up all wonted thought,
And scorns the care of our remaining woes;
 The sorrows, which themselves for us have
  wrought,

Are burnt to cinders by new kindled fires;
 The ashes are dispersed into the air;
The sighs, the groans of all our past desires
 Are clean outworn, as things that never were.

With youth is dead the hope of love's return,
 Who looks not back to hear our after-cries:
Where he is not, he laughs at those that mourn;
 Whence he is gone, he scorns the mind that dies.

When he is absent, he believes no words;
 When reason speaks, he, careless, stops his ears;
Whom he hath left, he never grace affords,
 But bathes his wings in our lamenting tears.

Unlasting passion, soon outworn conceit,
 Whereon I built, and on so dureless trust!

My mind had wounds, I dare not say deceit,
　Were I resolved her promise was not just.

Sorrow was my revenge and woe my hate;
　I powerless was to alter my desire;
My love is not of time or bound to date;
　My heart's internal heat and living fire

Would not, or could, be quenched with sudden
　　　　showers;
My bound respect was not confined to days;
My vowed faith not set to ended hours;
　I love the bearing and not bearing sprays

Which now to others do their sweetness send;
　The incarnate, snow-driven white, and purest
　　　azure,
Who from high heaven doth on their fields descend,
　Filling their barns with grain, and towers with
　　　treasure.

Erring or never erring, such is love
　As, while it lasteth, scorns the account of those
Seeking but self-contentment to improve,
　And hides, if any be, his inward woes,

And will not know, while he knows his own passion,
　The often and unjust perseverance
In deeds of love and state, and every action
　From that first day and year of their joy's entrance.

But I, unblessed and ill-born creature,
　That did embrace the dust her body bearing,
That loved her, both by fancy and by nature,
　That drew, even with the milk in my first sucking,

Affection from the parent's breast that bare me,
   Have found her as a stranger so severe,
Improving my mishap in each degree ;
   But love was gone : so would I my life were !

A queen she was to me,—no more Belphœbe ;
   A lion then,—no more a milk-white dove ;
A prisoner in her breast I could not be ;—
   She did untie the gentle chains of love.

      *   *   *   *   *
Love was no more the love of hiding

All trespass and mischance for her own glory :
   It had been such ; it was still for the elect ;
But I must be the example in love's story ;
   This was of all forepast the sad effect.

But thou, my weary soul and heavy thought,
   Made by her love a burthen to my being,
Dost know my error never was forethought,
   Or ever could proceed from sense of loving.

Of other cause if then it had proceeding,
   I leave the excuse, sith judgment hath been
      given ;
The limbs divided, sundered, and ableeding,
   Cannot complain the sentence was uneven.

This did that nature's wonder, virtue's choice,
   The only paragon of time's begetting,
Divine in words, angelical in voice,
   That spring of joys, that flower of love's own
      setting,

The idea remaining of those golden ages,
    That beauty, braving heavens and earth em-
        balming,
Which after worthless worlds but play on stages,
    Such didst thou her long since describe, yet
        sighing

That thy unable spirit could not find aught,
    In heaven's beauties or in earth's delight,
For likeness fit to satisfy thy thought:
    But what hath it availed thee so to write?

She cares not for thy praise, who knows not theirs;
    It's now an idle labour, and a tale
Told out of time, that dulls the hearer's ears:
    A merchandize whereof there is no sale.

Leave them, or lay them up with thy despairs!
    She hath resolved, and judged thee long ago.
Thy lines are now a murmuring to her ears,
    Like to a falling stream, which, passing slow,

Is wont to nourish sleep and quietness;
    So shall thy painful labours be perused,
And draw on rest, which sometime had regard;
    But those her cares thy errors have excused.

Thy days fordone have had their day's reward;
    So her hard heart, so her estranged mind,
In which above the heavens I once reposed;
    So to thy error have her ears inclined,

And have forgotten all thy past deserving,
    Holding in mind but only thine offence;
And only now affecteth thy depraving,
    And thinks all vain that pleadeth thy defence.

Yet greater fancy beauty never bred;
　　A more desire the heart-blood never nourished;
Her sweetness an affection never fed,
　　Which more in any age hath ever flourished.

The mind and virtue never have begotten
　　A firmer love, since love on earth had power;
A love obscured, but cannot be forgotten;
　　Too great and strong for time's jaws to devour;

Containing such a faith as ages wound not,
　　Care, wakeful ever of her good estate,
Fear, dreading loss, which sighs and joys not.
　　A memory of the joys her grace begat;

A lasting gratefulness for those comforts past,
　　Of which the cordial sweetness cannot die;
These thoughts, knit up by faith, shall ever last;
　　These time assays, but never can untie,

Whose life once lived in her pearl-like breast.
　　Whose joys were drawn but from her happiness.
Whose heart's high pleasure, and whose mind's
　　　　true rest,
　　Proceeded from her fortune's blessedness;

Who was intentive, wakeful, and dismayed
　　In fears, in dreams, in feverous jealousy,
Who long in silence served, and obeyed
　　With secret heart and hidden loyalty,

Which never change to sad adversity,
　　Which never age, or nature's overthrow,
Which never sickness or deformity,
　　Which never wasting care or wearing woe,
If subject unto these she could have been,—

Which never words or wits malicious,
   Which never honour's bait, or world's fame,
Achieved by attempts adventurous,
   Or aught beneath the sun or heaven's frame

Can so dissolve, dissever, or destroy
   The essential love of no frail parts compounded,
Though of the same now buried be the joy,
   The hope, the comfort, and the sweetness ended,

But that the thoughts and memories of these
   Work a relapse of passion, and remain
Of my sad heart the sorrow-sucking bees;
   The wrongs received, the frowns persuade in vain.

And though these medicines work desire to end,
   And are in others the true cure of liking,
The salves that heal love's wounds, and do amend
   Consuming woe, and slake our hearty sighing,

They work not so in thy mind's long decease;
   External fancy time alone recureth:
All whose effects do wear away with ease
   Love of delight, while such delight endureth;
Stays by the pleasure, but no longer stays . . . .

But in my mind so is her love inclosed,
   And is thereof not only the best part,
But into it the essence is disposed:
   Oh love! (the more my woe) to it thou art

Even as the moisture in each plant that grows;
   Even as the sun unto the frozen ground;
Even as the sweetness to the incarnate rose;
   Even as the centre in each perfect round:

As water to the fish, to men as air,
    As heat to fire, as light unto the sun ;
Oh love ! it is but vain to say thou *were ;*
    Ages and times cannot thy power outrun.

Thou art the soul of that unhappy mind
    Which, being by nature made an idle thought,
Began even then to take immortal kind,
    When first her virtues in thy spirits wrought.

From thee therefore that mover cannot move,
    Because it is become thy cause of being ;
Whatever error may obscure that love,
    Whatever frail effect in mortal living,

Whatever passion from distempered heart,
    What absence, time, or injuries effect,
What faithless friends or deep dissembled art
    Present to feed her most unkind suspect.

                *   *   *   *   *   *

Yet as the air in deep caves underground
    Is strongly drawn when violent heat hath vent,
Great clefts therein, till moisture do abound,
    And then the same, imprisoned and uppent,

Breaks out in earthquakes tearing all asunder ;
    So, in the centre of my cloven heart—
My heart, to whom her beauties were such wonder—
    Lies the sharp poisoned head of that love's dart

Which, till all break and all dissolve to dust,
    Thence drawn it cannot be, or therein known :
There, mixed with my heart-blood, the fretting rust
    The better part hath eaten and outgrown.

But what of those or these? or what of ought
   Of that which was, or that which is, to treat?
What I possess is but the same I sought:
   My love was false, my labours were deceit.

Nor less than such they are esteemed to be;
   A fraud bought at the price of many woes;
A guile, whereof the profits unto me—
   Could it be thought premeditate for those?

Witness those withered leaves left on the tree,
   The sorrow-worn face, the pensive mind;
The external shews what may the internal be:
   Cold care hath bitten both the root and rind.

But stay, my thoughts, make end: give fortune way:
   Harsh is the voice of woe and sorrow's sound:
Complaints cure not, and tears do but allay
   Griefs for a time, which after more abound.

To seek for moisture in the Arabian sand
   Is but a loss of labour and of rest:
The links which time did break of hearty bands

Words cannot knit, or wailings make anew.
   Seek not the sun in clouds when it is set. . . .
On highest mountains, where those cedars grew,
   Against whose banks the troubled ocean beat,

And were the marks to find thy hoped port,
   Into a soil far off themselves remove.
On Sestus' shore, Leander's late resort,
   Hero hath left no lamp to guide her love.

Thou lookest for light in vain, and storms arise;
   She sleeps thy death, that erst thy danger sighed;

E

Strive then no more ; bow down thy weary eyes—
  Eyes which to all these woes thy heart have
    guided.

She is gone, she is lost, she is found, she is ever fair :
  Sorrow draws weakly, where love draws not too :
Woe's cries sound nothing, but only in love's ear.
  Do then by dying what life cannot do.

Unfold thy flocks and leave them to the fields,
  To feed on hills, or dales, where likes them best,
Of what the summer or the spring-time yields,
  For love and time hath given thee leave to rest.

Thy heart which was their fold, now in decay
  By often storms and winter's many blasts,
All torn and rent becomes misfortune's prey ;
  False hope my shepherd's staff, now age hath
    brast

My pipe, which love's own hand gave my desire
  To sing her praises and my woe upon,—
Despair hath often threatened to the fire,
  As vain to keep now all the rest are gone.

Thus home I draw, as death's long night draws on ;
  Yet every foot, old thoughts turn back mine eyes:
Constraint me guides, as old age draws a stone
  Against the hill, which over-weighty lies

For feeble arms or wasted strength to move :
  My steps are backward, gazing on my loss,
My mind's affection and my soul's sole love,
  Not mixed with fancy's chaff or fortune's dross.

To God I leave it, who first gave it me,
    And I her gave, and she returned again,
As it was hers ; so let His mercies be
    Of my last comforts the essential mean.

But be it so or not, the effects are past ;
Her love hath end ; my woe must ever last.

The end of the books of the " Ocean's Love to Cynthia,"
and the beginning of the 22nd book, entreating of Sorrow.

My days' delights, my spring-time joys fordone,
Which in the dawn and rising sun of youth
    Had their creation, and were first begun,

Do in the evening and the winter sad
Present my mind, which takes my time's account,
    The grief remaining of the joy it had.

My times that then ran o'er themselves in these,
And now run out in other's happiness,
    Bring unto those new joys and new-born days.

So could she not if she were not the sun,
    Which sees the birth and burial of all else,
And holds that power with which she first begun,

    Leaving each withered body to be torn
By fortune, and by times tempestuous,
    Which, by her virtue, once fair fruit have born ;

    Knowing she can renew, and can create
Green from the ground, and flowers even out of stone,
    By virtue lasting over time and date,

    Leaving us only woe, which, like the moss,
Having compassion of unburied bones,
    Cleaves to mischance, and unrepaired loss.

    For tender stalks—

(MS. abruptly ends here.)

XXI.

SIR WALTER RALEIGH'S PETITION TO THE QUEEN

(ANNE OF DENMARK).[1]

(1618.)

 HAD truth power, the guiltless could
  not fall,
Malice win glory, or revenge triumph ;
 But truth alone cannot encounter all.

Mercy is fled to God, which mercy made ;
Compassion dead ; faith turned to policy ;
 Friends know not those who sit in sorrow's shade.

For what we sometime were, we are no more :
Fortune hath changed our shape, and destiny
 Defaced the very form we had before.

All love, and all desert of former times,
Malice hath covered from my sovereign's eyes,
 And largely laid abroad supposed crimes.

But kings call not to mind what vassals were,
But know them now, as envy hath described them :
 So can I look on no side from despair.

[1] Hawthornden MSS. in the Library of the Antiquarian
Society of Scotland; vol. viii. "Drummond Miscellanies,"
II. First printed by Mr. D. Laing in "Archæol. Scot.,"
vol. iv. pp. 236-8. The original title runs: "S. W.
Raghlies Petition to the Queene. 1618."

Cold walls! to you I speak; but you are senseless:
Celestial Powers! you hear, but have determined,
   And shall determine, to my greatest happiness.

Then unto whom shall I unfold my wrong,
Cast down my tears, or hold up folded hands?
   To Her, to whom remorse doth most belong;

To Her who is the first, and may alone
Be justly called the Empress of the Bretanes.
   Who should have mercy if a Queen have none?

Save those that would have died for your defence!
Save him whose thoughts no treason ever tainted!
   For lo! destruction is no recompense.

If I have sold my duty, sold my faith
To strangers, which was only due to One;
   Nothing I should esteem so dear as death.

But if both God and Time shall make you know
That I, your humblest vassal, am oppressed,
   Then cast your eyes on undeserved woe;

That I and mine may never mourn the miss
Of Her we had, but praise our living Queen,
   Who brings us equal, if not greater, bliss.

XXII.

SIR WALTER RALEIGH'S VERSES,

FOUND IN HIS BIBLE IN THE GATE-HOUSE AT WESTMINSTER.[1]

(1618.)

EVEN such is time, that takes in trust
 Our youth, our joys, our all we have,
And pays us but with earth and dust;
 Who, in the dark and silent grave,
When we.have wandered all our ways,
Shuts up the story of our days;
But from this earth, this grave, this dust,
My God shall raise me up, I trust!

W. R.

[1] Printed with Raleigh's " Prerogative of Parliaments," 1628, and probably still earlier; also with " To-day a Man, To-morrow none," 1643-4; in Raleigh's " Remains," 1661, &c., with the title given above; and in " Rel. Wotton." 1651, &c., with the title, " Sir Walter Raleigh the night before his death." Also found with several variations in many old MS. copies.

XXIII.

FRAGMENTS AND EPIGRAMS.

I.

THIS made him write in a glass window, obvious to the Queen's eye—

"'Fain would I climb, yet fear I to fall.'

Her Majesty, either espying or being shown it, did under-write—

"'If thy heart fails thee, climb not at all.'"[1]

II.

"Sir Wa. Rawley made this rhyme upon the name of a gallant, one Mr. Noel:—

"Noe. L.

"'The word of denial and the letter of fifty
Makes the gentleman's name that will never be thrifty.'

"And Noel's answer:—

"'Raw. Ly.

"The foe to the stomach and the word of disgrace
Shews the gentleman's name with the bold face.'"[2]

---

[1] Fuller, "Worthies of England," Devonshire, p. 261.
[2] Manningham's "Diary," under date Dec. 30, 1602; Camden Society edition, p. 109; and Collier's "Hist. Dram. Poetry," i. 336, note. Somewhat different in MS. Malone 19, p. 42.

III.

In vain mine eyes, in vain you waste your tears ;
In vain my sighs, the smokes of my despairs ;
In vain you search the earth and heavens above ;
In vain ye seek ; for Fortune keeps my love.[1]

IV.

WITH wisdom's eyes had but blind fortune seen,
Then had my love, my love for ever been.[2]

V.

EPITAPH ON THE EARL OF LEICESTER.[3]
(Died Sept. 4, 1588.)

HERE lies the noble warrior that never blunted
    sword ;
Here lies the noble courtier that never kept his
    word ;
Here lies his excellency that governed all the state ;
Here lies the L. of Leicester that all the world did
    hate.

WA. RA.

VI.

EPITAPH ON THE EARL OF SALISBURY.[4]
(Died May 24, 1612.)

HERE lies Hobbinol, our pastor whilere,
That once in a quarter our fleeces did sheer.

---

[1] Puttenham's " Art of English Poesie," 1589, p. 165,
as " this written by Sir Walter Raleigh of his greatest
mistress in most excellent verses."

[2] Puttenham, *ibid.*, p. 167, as " that of Sir Walter
Raleigh's very sweet."

[3] Collier's " Bibliographical Catalogue," vol. ii. p. 222,
from a Bridgewater MS. It is anonymous in the Hawthorn-
den MSS. ; and in a shorter form in MS. Ashm. 38, p. 181.

[4] Shirley's " Life of Raleigh," p. 28, folio.

To please us his cur he kept under clog,
And was ever after both shepherd and dog.
For oblation to Pan his custom was thus :—
He first gave a trifle, then offered up us.
And through his false worship such power he did
      gain,
As kept him o' th' mountain and us on the plain :
Where many a hornpipe he tuned to his Phyllis,
And sweetly sung Walsingham to 's Amaryllis.

(Two lines omitted.)

VII.

A Poem put into my Lady Laiton's Pocket

by Sir Walter Raleigh.[1]

Lady, farewell, whom I in silence serve !
  Would God thou knewest the depth of my desire !
Then mought I wish, though nought I can deserve,
  Some drops of grace to slake my scalding fire ;
But sith to live alone I have decreed,
I'll spare to speak, that I may spare to speed !

VIII.

Sir W. Raleigh on the Snuff of a Candle

the Night before he Died.[2]

Cowards [may] fear to die ; but courage stout,
Rather than live in snuff, will be put out.

---

[1] Chetham MS., 8012, p. 85 ; erased, but still legible.
[2] Raleigh's " Remains," p. 253, edition 1661, &c.

XXIV.

METRICAL TRANSLATIONS

OCCURRING IN SIR W. RALEIGH'S HISTORY OF
THE WORLD.

I. BOOK I. CH. I. § 6.
Virgil, Æneid, vi. 724-7.

THE heaven and earth and all the liquid
    main,
    The moon's bright globe and stars
        Titanian,
A spirit within maintains; and their whole mass
A mind, which through each part infused doth pass,
Fashions and works, and wholly doth transpierce
All this great body of the universe.

II. BOOK I. CH. I. § 7.
Ovid, Metam. iv. 226-8.

THE world discerns itself, while I the world behold;
By me the longest years and other times are told;
I, the world's eye.

III. BOOK I. CH. I. § 11.
Ovid, Trist. iii. vi. 18; and Juvenal, vii. 201.

'GAINST fate no counsel can prevail.
    Kingdoms to slaves by destiny,
    To captives triumphs given be.

IV. BOOK I. CH. I. § 15.

Athenæus (? Agathon: cf. Ar. Eth. N. vi. 4).

FROM wisdom fortune differs far ;
And yet in works most like they are.

V. BOOK I. CH. I. § 15.

Ovid, Remed. Am. 119.

WHILE fury gallops on the way,
Let no man fury's gallop stay.

VI. BOOK I. CH. II. § 1.

Ovid, Metam. i. 76-8.

MORE holy than the rest, and understanding more,
A living creature wants, to rule all made before;
So man began to be.

VII. BOOK I. CH. II. § 3.

Marius Victor, de perversis suæ æt. moribus Epist. 30-33.

DISEASES, famine, enemies, in us no change have
          wrought ;
What erst we were, we are ; still in the same snare
          caught :
  No time can our corrupted manners mend ;
  In vice we dwell, in sin that hath no end.

VIII. BOOK I. CH. II. § 5.

Ovid, Metam. i. 414-5.

FROM thence our kind hard-hearted is, enduring
    pain and care;
Approving that our bodies of a stony nature are.

IX. BOOK I. CH. II. § 5.

Albinovanus, Eleg. de ob. Mæc. 113-4.

THE plants and trees made poor and old
    By winter envious,
    The spring-time bounteous
Covers again from shame and cold ;
But never man repaired again
    His youth and beauty lost,
    Though art and care and cost
Do promise nature's help in vain.

X. BOOK I. CH. II. § 5.

Catull. Carm. v. 4-6.

THE sun may set and rise ;
But we, contrariwise,
Sleep after our short light
One everlasting night.

XI. BOOK I. CH. III. § 3.

Ovid, Metam. I. 61-2.

THE East wind with Aurora hath abiding
    Among the Arabian and the Persian hills,
Whom Phœbus first salutes at his uprising.

XII. BOOK I. CH. III. § 3.

Ovid, Metam. I. 107-8.

THE joyful spring did ever last, and Zephyrus did
    breed
Sweet flowers by his gentle blast, without the help
    of seed.

XIII. BOOK I. CH. IV. § 2.

Virgil, Æneid I. 490-1.

THE Amazon with crescent-formed shield
Penthesilea leads into the field.

XIV. BOOK I. CH. V. § 5.

Lucan, Pharsal. IV. 373-8, 380-1.

O WASTEFUL riot, never well content
    With low-priced fare; hunger ambitious
Of cates by land and sea far fetched and sent;
    Vain glory of a table sumptuous;
Learn with how little life may be preserved.
    In gold and myrrh they need not to carouse;
But with the brook the people's thirst is served,
Who, fed with bread and water, are not starved.

XV. BOOK I. CH. V. § 8.

John Cassam out of Orpheus, Fragm. L. from Etym. M.

.FROM the earth and from thy blood, O heaven, they
    came,
Whom thereupon the gods did giants name.

XVI. BOOK I. CH. VI. § 3.

Anaxandr. Rhod. ap. Natal. Com. I. 7; p. 12, ed. 1612.

I SACRIFICE to God the beef which you adore;
I broil the Egyptian eels, which you as God implore;
You fear to eat the flesh of swine; I find it sweet;
You worship dogs; to beat them I think meet,
When they my store devour.

XVII. BOOK I. CH. VI. § 3.

Juvenal, xv. 9-11.

THE Egyptians think it sin to root up or to bite
Their leeks or onions, which they serve with holy
 rite.
 O happy nations, which of their own sowing
 Have store of gods in every garden growing!

XVIII. BOOK I. CH. VI. § 4.

Ovid, Metam. I. 150.

ASTRÆA last of heavenly wights the earth did leave.

XIX. BOOK I. CH. VI. § 4.

Cornelius Severus, Ætna, 43-5.

THE giants did advance their wicked hand
 Against the stars, to thrust them headlong down;
 And, robbing Jove of his imperial crown,
On conquered heavens to lay their proud command.

XX. BOOK I. CH. VI. § 5.

Lycophron, Alexandr. 1200.

SATURN to be the fatter is not known,
By being the grave and burial of his own.

XXI. BOOK I. CH. VI. § 5.

Sibylla, III. p. 227, ed. Paris, 1599.

THINGS thus agreed, Titan made Saturn swear
  No son to nourish; which by reigning might
Usurp the right of Titan's lawful heir.

XXII. BOOK I. CH. VI. § 5.

Callim. εἰς τὸν Δία, 8, 9.

THE Cretans ever liars were; they care not what
    they say;
For they a tomb have built for thee, O king that
    livest alway.

XXIII. BOOK I. CH. VI. § 7.

Eurip. Fragm. Melanipp. vi. Dind.

HEAVEN and earth one form did bear;
But when disjoined once they were
    From mutual embraces,
All things to light appeared then;
Of trees, birds, beasts, fishes, and men
    The still remaining races.

XXIV. BOOK I. CH. VI. § 7.

Orpheus to Musæus; Fragm. i. from Just. Mart.,
Cohort. ad Gent. 15.

THEN marking this my sacred speech, but truly lend
Thy heart that's reason's sphere, and the right way
    ascend,
And see the world's sole king.   First, He is simply
    one
Begotten of Himself, from whom is born alone
All else, in which He's still; nor could it e'er befall
A mortal eye to see Him once, yet He sees all.

XXV. BOOK I. CH. VI. § 7.

Id. Fragm. vi. from Proclus.

THE first of all is God, and the same last is He.
God is the head and midst; yea, from Him all
    things be.
God is the base of earth and of the starred sky;
He is the male and female too; shall never die.
The spirit of all is God; the sun and moon and
    what is higher;
The king, the original of all, of all the end:
For close in holy breast He all did comprehend;
Whence all to blessed light His wondrous power
    did send.

XXVI. BOOK I. CH. VII. § 2.

Ovid, Metam. xv. 293-4.

BURA and Helice on Achaian ground
Are sought in vain, but under sea are found.

XXVII. BOOK I. CH. VII. § 3.

Virgil, Æneid, viii. 318-23.

SATURN descending from the heavens high,
　Fearing the arms of Jupiter his son,
His kingdom lost, and banished, thence doth fly.
　Rude people on the mountain tops he won
To live together, and by laws; which done,
　He chose to call it Latium.

XXVIII. BOOK I. CH. VII. § 3.

Virgil, Æneid, viii. 328.

THEN came the Ausonian bands and the Sicanian
　tribes.

XXIX. BOOK I. CH. VII. § 7.

Ovid, Fasti, i. 103-4.

THE ancients called me Chaos; my great years
By those old times of which I sing appears.

XXX. BOOK I. CH. VIII. § 3.

Tibull. Eleg. i. vii. 20.

TYRUS knew first how ships might use the wind.

XXXI. BOOK I. CH. VIII. § 3.

Lucan, Pharsal. iv. 131-5.

THE moistened osier of the hoary willow
　Is woven first into a little boat;

F

Then, clothed in bullock's hide, upon the billow
    Of a proud river lightly doth it float
        Under the waterman :
    So on the lakes of overswelling Po
    Sails the Venetian ; and the Briton so
        On the outspread ocean.

XXXII. BOOK I. CH. VIII. § 4.

Apollon. Rhod. Argonaut. II. 1004-6.

THE Chalybes plough not their barren soil,
    But undermine high hills for iron veins ;
Changing the purchase of their endless toil
    For merchandize, which their poor lives sustains.

XXXIII. BOOK I. CH. VIII. § II. † 2.

Ovid, Fasti, II. 289-90.

THE Arcadians the earth inhabited
Ere yet the moon did shine, or Jove was bred.

XXXIV. BOOK I. CH. X. § 2.

Ovid, Metam. IV. 57-8.

SEMIRAMIS with walls of brick the city did enclose.

XXXV. BOOK I. CH. X. § 7.

Sedulius, I. 226-31.

AH ! wretched they that worship vanities,
    And consecrate dumb idols in their heart ;
Who their own maker, God on high, despise,
    And fear the work of their own hands and art !

What fury, what great madness, doth beguile
  Men's minds, that man should ugly shapes adore,
Of birds or bulls or dragons, or the vile
  Half-dog, half-man, on knees for aid implore!

XXXVI. BOOK I. CH. XI. § 7.

Cic. De Divin. II. 56, et al.

  If Cœsus over Halys go,
  Great kingdoms he shall overthrow.

XXXVII. BOOK I. CH. XI. § 8.

Lucretius, II. 54-5.

We fear by light, as children in the dark.

XXXVIII. BOOK II. CH. VI. § 4.

Æschylus, P. V. 456-61.

But fortune governed all their works, till when
  I first found out how stars did set and rise,—
A profitable art to mortal men.
  And others of like use I did devise:
  As letters to compose in learned wise
I first did teach, and first did amplify
The mother of the Muses, Memory.

XXXIX. BOOK II. CH. VI. § 5.

Ovid, Metam. I. 322-3.

No man was better nor more just than he,
Nor any woman godlier than she.

XL. BOOK II. CH. VII. § 3. † 3.

Sidonius, Carm. xvii. 15, 16.

I HAVE no wine of Gaza nor Falerna wine,
Nor any for thy drinking of Sarepta's vine.

XLI. BOOK II, CH. VII. § 4. † 5.

Virgil, Georg. II. 448

OF yew the Ituræans' bows were made.

XLII. BOOK II. CH. VIII. § 1.

Virgil, Æneid, I. 728-30.

THE queen anon commands the weighty bowl,
Weighty with precious stones and massy gold,
To flow with wine.   This Belus used of old,
And all of Belus' line.

XLIII. BOOK II. CH. VIII. § 1.

Lucan, Pharsal. III. 220-1.

PHŒNICIANS first, if fame may credit have,
In rude characters dared our words to grave.

XLIV. BOOK II. CH. VIII. § 1.

Diog. Laert. VII. 30.

IF a Phœnician born I am, what then ?
Cadmus was so ; to whom Greece owes
The books of learned men.

XLV. BOOK II. CH. X. § 2.

Tibullus, I. vii. 18.

THE white dove is for holy held in Syria Palestine.

XLVI. BOOK II. CH. XIII. § 3.

Ovid, Am. II. ii. 43-4.

HERE Tantalus in water seeks for water, and doth
    miss
The fleeting fruit he catcheth at; his long tongue
    brought him this.

XLVII. BOOK II. CH. XIII. § 3.

Horace, Sat. I. i. 68-70.

THE thirsting Tantalus doth catch at streams that
    from him flee;
Why laughest thou? The name but changed, the
    tale is told of thee.

XLVIII. BOOK II. CH. XIII. §

Natalis Com. p. 627, ed. 1612, out of Pindar, Ol. i. 60-63.

BECAUSE that, stealing immortality,
He did both nectar and ambrosia give
To guests of his own age to make them live.

XLIX. BOOK II. CH. XIII. § 3.

Tibullus, I. iii. 75-6, out of Homer, Od. xi. 576.

NINE furlongs stretched lies Tityus, who for his
    wicked deeds
The hungry birds with his renewing liver daily
    feeds.

L. BOOK II. CH. XIII. § 3.

Ovid, Heroid. xvi. 179-80.

STRONG Ilion thou shalt see with walls and towers
        high,
Built with the harp of wise Apollo's harmony.

LI. BOOK II. CH. XIII. § 4.

Horace, Od. III. xvi. 1-11.

THE brazen tower, with doors close barred,
And watchful bandogs' frightful guard,
        Kept safe the maidenhead
Of Danae from secret love,
Till smiling Venus and wise Jove
        Beguiled her father's dread :
For, changed into a golden shower,
The god into her lap did pour
        Himself and took his pleasure.
Through guards and stony walls to break,
The thunderbolt is far more weak
        Than is a golden treasure.

LII. BOOK II. CH. XIII. § 8.

Lucretius, v. 325-8.

IF all this world had no original,
    But things have ever been as now they are
Before the siege of Thebes or Troy's last fall,
    Why did no poet sing some elder war?

LIII. BOOK II. CH. XIV. § 1.

Virgil, Æneid, III. 104-12.

In the main sea the isle of Crete doth lie,
Whence Jove was born; thence is our progeny.
There is Mount Ida; there in fruitful land
An hundred great and goodly cities stand.
Thence, if I follow not mistaken fame,
Teucer, the eldest of our grandsires, came
To the Rhœtean shores, and reigned there
Ere yet fair Ilion was built, and ere
The towers of Troy.   Their dwelling-place they
   sought
In lowest vales.   Hence Cybel's rites were brought;
Hence Corybantian cymbals did remove;
And hence the name of our Idæan grove.

LIV. BOOK II. CH. XIV. § 1.

Virgil, Æneid, III. 163-8.

Hesperia the Grecians call the place,—
An ancient fruitful land, a warlike race.
Œnotrians held it; now the later progeny
Gives it their captain's name, and calls it Italy.
This seat belongs to us; hence Dardanus,
Hence came the author of our stock, Iasius.

LV. BOOK II. CH. XIV. § 1.

Virgil, Æneid, VII. 205-11.

Some old Auruncans, I remember well—
Though time have made the fame obscure—would
   tell

Of Dardanus, how born in Italy ;
From hence he into Phrygia did fly.
And leaving Tuscane, where he erst had place,
With Corythus did sail to Samothrace ;
But now enthronized he sits on high,
In golden palace of the starry sky.

LVI. BOOK II. CH. XIV. § 1.

Horace, Od. IV. ix. 25-8.

MANY by valour have deserved renown
  Ere Agamemnon, yet lie all oppressed
Under long night, unwept for and unknown ;
  For with no sacred poet were they blest.

LVII. BOOK II. CH. XXI. § 6.

Horace, Od. III. iv. 45-8.

WHO rules the duller earth, the wind-swollen
      streams,
The civil cities and the infernal realms,
Who the host of heaven and the mortal band
Alone doth govern by his just command.

LVIII. BOOK II. CH. XXII. § 6.

Ausonius, Epigr. CXVIII.

I AM that Dido which thou here dost see,
Cunningly framed in beauteous imagery.
Like this I was, but had not such a soul
As Maro feigned. incestuous and foul.
Æneas never with his Trojan host
Beheld my face, or landed on this coast.

But flying proud Iarbas' villainy—
Not moved by furious love or jealousy—
I did, with weapon chaste, to save my fame,
Make way for death untimely ere it came.
This was my end.   But first I built a town,
Revenged my husband's death, lived with renown.
Why didst thou stir up Virgil, envious Muse,
Falsely my name and honour to abuse?
Readers, believe historians; not those
Which to the world Jove's thefts and vice expose.
Poets are liars; and for verses' sake,
Will make the gods of human crimes partake.

LIX. BOOK II. CH. XXIII. § 4.

Horace, Od. III. xxiv. 36-41.

Nor southern heat nor northern snow, .
That freezing to the ground doth grow,
The subject regions can fence,
And keep the greedy merchant thence.
The subtle shipmen way will find,
Storm never so the seas with wind.

LX. BOOK II. CH. XXIII. § 5.

Horace, Od. IV. ii. 17, 18.

Such as like heavenly wights do come
With an Elean garland home.

LXI. BOOK II. CH. XXIV. § 1.   (Compare No. LIV.)

Virgil, Æneid, I. 530-3.

There is a land which Greeks Hesperia name,
Ancient and strong, of much fertility;

Œnotrians held it; but we hear by fame,
  That, by late ages of posterity,
  'Tis from a captain's name called Italy.

LXII. BOOK II. CH. XXIV. § 5.

Juvenal, viii. 272-5.

YET, though thou fetch thy pedigree so far,
Thy first progenitor, whoe'er he were,
Some shepherd was; or else—that I'll forbear.

LXIII. BOOK III. CH. VII. § 3.

Horace, Od. III. ii. 31-2.

SELDOM the villain, though much haste he make,
Lame-footed vengeance fails to overtake.

LXIV. BOOK IV. CH. I. § 5.

Horace, Od. III. xvi. 13-15.

BY gifts the Macedon clave gates asunder,
The kings envying his estate brought under.

LXV. BOOK IV. CH. II. § 8.

Homer, Od. XVIII. 135-6.

THE minds of men are ever so affected
As by God's will they daily are directed.

LXVI. BOOK IV. CH. II. § 15.

Claudian in Eutrop. I. 321-3.

OVER the Medes and light Sabæans reigns
  This female sex; and under arms of Queen
Great part of the Barbarian land remains.

LXVII. BOOK V. CH. II. § 1.

Juvenal, VIII. 121-2.

HAVE special care that valiant poverty
Be not oppressed with too great injury.

LXVIII. BOOK V. CH. VI. § 11.

Pausan. (VII) XII. vol. iii. p. 182, Siebelis.

ONE fire than other burns more forcibly;
  One wolf than other wolves does bite more sore;
One hawk than other hawks more swift doth fly;
  So one most mischievous of men before,
Callicrates, false knave as knave might be,
Met with Menalcidas, more false than he.[1]

LXIX. BOOK V. CH. VI. § 12.

Juvenal, x. 96-7.

EVEN they that have no murderous will
Would have it in their power to kill.

---

[1] "A bye-word, taken up among the Achæans, whenas that mischievous Callicrates, who had been too hard for all worthy and virtuous men, was beaten at his own weapon, by one of his own condition."

XXV.[1]

NO PLEASURE WITHOUT PAIN.[2]

(Before 1576.)

SWEET were the joys that both might
        like and last;
    Strange were the state exempt from
        all distress;
Happy the life that no mishap should taste;
    Blessed the chance might never change success.
Were such a life to lead or state to prove,
Who would not wish that such a life were love?

But oh! the soury sauce of sweet unsure,
    When pleasures flit, and fly with waste of wind·
The trustless trains that hoping hearts allure,
    When sweet delights do but allure the mind;
When care consumes and wastes the wretched wight,
While fancy feeds and draws of her delight.

[1] This and the next five poems are placed last, because I
cannot satisfy myself that the evidence is conclusive in
Raleigh's favour. But I do not exclude them altogether,
because in each case there is some evidence which others
have accepted, and no stronger claim has been set up for any
other person.
[2] "Paradise of Dainty Devices," 1576, signed "W. R."
in ed. 1578; see Collier's reprint, p. 20, and "Bibl. Cat.,"
vol. i. p. 245; signed "W. Hunnis" in editions 1580 and
1596, where it is No. 12; in other editions signed "E. S."

What life were love, if love were free from pain ?
   But oh that pain with pleasure matched should
      meet !
Why did the course of nature so ordain
   That sugared sour must sauce the bitter sweet ?
Which sour from sweet might any means remove,
What hap, what heaven, what life, were like to love !

XXVI.

THE SHEPHERD'S PRAISE OF HIS SACRED DIANA.[1]

Before 1593.)

RAISED be Diana's fair and harmless
      light;
     Praised be the dews wherewith she
      moists the ground ;
Praised be her beams, the glory of the night ;
   Praised be her power, by which all powers abound.

Praised be her nymphs, with whom she decks the
     woods ;
   Praised be her knights, in whom true honour lives ;

[1] In "England's Helicon," 1600, Raleigh's initials were first affixed, but were obliterated by pasting over them a slip of paper with the word "Ignoto." The piece is marked "W. R." in F. Davison's catalogue of the poems contained in "England's Helicon," Harl. MS. 280, fol. 99. It is anonymous in the "Phœnix Nest," 1593, p. 69.

Praised be that force, by which she moves the floods;
  Let that Diana shine which all these gives.

In heaven queen she is among the spheres;
  She mistress-like makes all things to be pure:
Eternity in her oft change she bears;
  She beauty is; by her the fair endure.

Time wears her not; she doth his chariot guide;
  Mortality below her orb is placed;
By her the virtues of the stars down slide;
  In her is virtue's perfect image cast.

A knowledge pure it is her worth to know:
With Circes let them dwell that think not so.

[S. W. R.] IGNOTO.

XXVII.

THE SHEPHERD'S DESCRIPTION OF LOVE.[1]

(Before 1600.)

Melibœus.

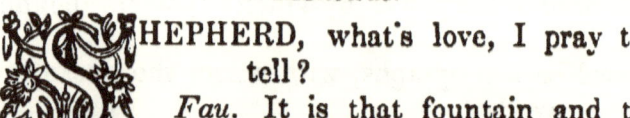 HEPHERD, what's love, I pray thee
    tell?
    Fau. It is that fountain and that
    well
Where pleasure and repentance dwell:
It is perhaps that saucing bell

---

[1] In " England's Helicon," 1600, with the first signature
obliterated, as in No. xxvi., and ascribed to "S. W.
Rawly" in F. Davison's list, Harl. MS. 280, fol. 99. It is

That tolls all into heaven or hell ;
And this is love as I heard tell.

Meli. Yet what is love, I prithee say ?
Fau. It is a work on holiday ;
It is December matched with May,
When lusty bloods, in fresh array,
    Hear ten months after of the play ;
    And this is love as I hear say.

Meli. Yet what is love, good shepherd, sain ?
Fau. It is a sunshine mixed with rain ;
It is a tooth-ache, or like pain ;
It is a game where none doth gain ;
    The lass saith no, and would full fain ;
    And this is love, as I hear sain.

Meli. Yet, shepherd, what is love, I pray ?
Fau. It is a yea, it is a nay,
A pretty kind of sporting fray ;
It is a thing will soon away ;
    Then, nymphs, take 'vantage while ye may ;
    And this is love, as I hear say.

Meli. Yet what is love, good shepherd, show ?
Fau. A thing that creeps ; it cannot go ;
A prize that passeth to and fro ;
A thing for one, a thing for moe ;
    And he that proves shall find it so ;
    And, shepherd, this is love, I trow.
                    [S. W. R.] Ignoto.

anonymous in Davison's " Poetical Rhapsody," 1602, &c.,
as " The Anatomy of Love," with no distinction of dialogue,
and the first line running, "Now what is love, I pray thee
tell ? " An imperfect copy of the first and last stanzas form
" the third song " in T. Heywood's " Rape of Lucrece,"
1608, &c.

XXVIII.

AS YOU CAME FROM THE HOLY LAND.[1]

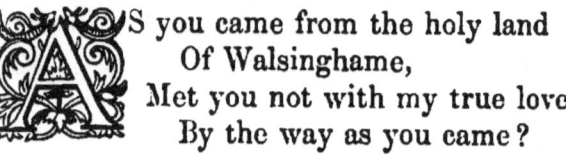S you came from the holy land
Of Walsinghame,
Met you not with my true love
By the way as you came?

How shall I know your true love,
That have met many one,
As I went to the holy land,
That have come, that have gone?

She is neither white nor brown,
But as the heavens fair;
There is none hath a form so divine
In the earth or the air.

Such a one did I meet, good sir,
Such an angelic face,
Who like a queen, like a nymph, did appear,
By her gate, by her grace.

[1] MS. Rawl. 85, fol. 124; signed as *infra*, and hence claimed for Raleigh by Dr. Bliss, Wood's " A. O.," vol. ii., p. 248, and inserted in the Oxford edition of Raleigh's " Works," vol. viii. p. 733, with the title " False Love and True Love." There is an anonymous copy in Percy's MS., vol. iii., p. 465, ed. Furnivall: and it is also in Deloney's " Garland of Goodwill," p. 111, Percy Society reprint.

She hath left me here all alone,
  All alone, as unknown,
Who sometimes did me lead with herself,
  And me loved as her own.

What's the cause that she leaves you alone,
  And a new way doth take,
Who loved you once as her own,
  And her joy did you make?

I have loved her all my youth,
  But now old, as you see:
Love likes not the falling fruit
  From the withered tree.

Know that Love is a careless child,
  And forgets promise past;
He is blind, he is deaf when he list,
  And in faith never fast.

His desire is a dureless content,
  And a trustless joy;
He is won with a world of despair,
  And is lost with a toy.

Of womenkind such indeed is the love,
  Or the word love abused,
Under which many childish desires
  And conceits are excused.

But true love is a durable fire,
  In the mind ever burning,
Never sick, never old, never dead,
  From itself never turning.

                    SR. W. R.

G

XXIX.

A POEM BY SIR WALTER RALEIGH.[1]

SHALL I, like an hermit, dwell
On a rock or in a cell,
Calling home the smallest part
That is missing of my heart,
To bestow it, where I may
Meet a rival every day?
  If she undervalue me,
  What care I how fair she be?

Were her tresses angel-gold,
If a stranger may be bold
Unrebuked, unafraid,
To convert them to a braid,
And, with little more ado,
Work them into bracelets too;
  If the mine be grown so free,
  What care I how rich it be?

Were her hand as rich a prize
As her hairs or precious eyes,
If she lay them out to take
Kisses for good manners' sake,
And let every lover skip
From her hand unto her lip;
  If she seem not chaste to me,
  What care I how chaste she be?

[1] "London Magazine," August. 1734, p. 444, entitled as
above. Mentioned on that authority only, by Oldys and
(apparently) Ritson, and appended to Raleigh's "Life" by
Cayley.

No; she must be perfect snow,
In effect as well as show;
Warming but as snow-balls do,
Not, like fire, by burning too;
But when she by change hath got
To her heart a second lot,
    Then, if others share with me,
    Farewell her, whate'er she be!

XXX.

TO HIS SINGULAR FRIEND,

WILLIAM LITHGOW.[1]

(1618.)

WHILES I admire thy first and second
        ways,
    Long ten years wandering in the
        world-wide bounds;
I rest amazed to think on these assays
    That thy first travel to the world forth sounds:
In bravest sense, compendious ornate style,
Didst show most rare adventures to this isle.

And now thy second pilgrimage I see
    At London thou resolvest to put in light;
Thy Libyan ways, so fearful to the eye,
    And Garamants their strange amazing sight.

[1] Prefixed to Lithgow's " Pilgrim's Farewell," 1618.

Meanwhile this work affords a´three-fold gain
In fury of thy fierce Castalian vein ;
As thou for travels brookest the greatest name,
So voyage on, increase, maintain the same !

W. R.

PART II

POEMS FROM

RELIQUIÆ WOTTONIANÆ,

1651-1685,

WITH SOME ADDITIONS.

POEMS FROM

RELIQUIÆ WOTTONIANÆ.

I.

A POEM WRITTEN BY SIR HENRY WOTTON

IN HIS YOUTH.[1]

(Before 1602.)

FAITHLESS world, and thy most
    faithless part,
      A woman's heart!
The true shop of variety, where sits
    Nothing but fits
And fevers of desire, and pangs of love,
    Which toys remove.
Why was she born to please? or I to trust
    Words writ in dust,
Suffering her eyes to govern my despair,
    My pain for air;

---

[1] "Rel. Wotton." Also in Davison's "Poetical Rhapsody,"
1602, &c., with Wotton's initials, as "an Elegy." In ed.
1621, p. 202, it has the longer title, "Of a Woman's Heart."
Wrongly claimed for Rudyard in the "Poems of Pembroke
and Rudyard," 1660, p. 34. A copy in MS. Rawl. Poet.
147, p. 74, signed "H. Wotton."

And fruit of time rewarded with untruth,
  The food of youth?
Untrue she was; yet I believed her eyes,
  Instructed spies,
Till I was taught, that love was but a school
  To breed a fool.
Or sought she more, by triumphs of denial,
  To make a trial   '
How far her smiles commanded my weakness?
  Yield, and confess!
Excuse no more thy folly; but, for cure,
  Blush and endure
As well thy shame as passions that were vain;
  And think, 'tis gain,
To know that love lodged in a woman's breast,
  Is but a guest.

          H. W.

II.

SIR HENRY WOTTON AND SERJEANT HOSKINS RIDING ON THE WAY.[1]

Hoskins.

NOBLE, lovely, virtuous creature,
  Purposely so framed by nature,
   To enthral your servant's wits:
  Wo. Time must now unite our hearts,
Not for any my deserts,
  But because methinks it fits.

   [1] "Rel. Wotton."

Ho. Dearest treasure of my thought,
  And yet wert thou to be bought
   With my life thou wert not dear:
Wo. Secret comfort of my mind,
  Doubt no longer to be kind,
   But be so, and so appear.

Ho. Give me love for love again;
  Let our loves be clear and plain;
   Heaven is fairest, when 'tis clearest:
Wo. Lest in clouds and in differing,
  We resemble seamen erring,
   Farthest off when we are nearest.

Ho. Thus with numbers interchanged,
  Wotton's muse and mine have ranged;
   Verse and journey both are spent:
Wo. And if Hoskins chance to say,
  That we well have spent the day,
   I, for my part, am content.

         H. W.

III.

THE CHARACTER OF A HAPPY LIFE.[1]

(*Circ.* 1614.)

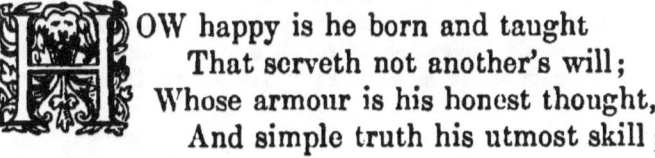 OW happy is he born and taught
  That serveth not another's will;
  Whose armour is his honest thought,
  And simple truth his utmost skill;

[1] " Rel. Wotton." Said to have been printed in 1614, with
Overbury's " Wife," &c.; traced at Dulwich with the date

Whose passions not his masters are ;
    Whose soul is still prepared for death,
Untied unto the world by care
    Of public fame or private breath ;

Who envies none that chance doth raise,
    Nor vice ; who never understood
How deepest wounds are given by praise ;
    Nor rules of state, but rules of good ;

Who hath his life from rumours freed ;
    Whose conscience is his strong retreat ;
Whose state can neither flatterers feed,
    Nor ruin make oppressors great ;

Who God doth late and early pray
    More of his grace than gifts to lend ;
And entertains the harmless day
    With a religious book or friend.

This man is freed from servile bands
    Of hope to rise or fear to fall :
Lord of himself, though not of lands,
    And, having nothing, yet hath all.

H. WOTTON.

1616 ; and quoted as Wotton's to Drummond by Ben Jonson
in 1619.   Mr. Collier has printed a copy from Ben Jonson's
handwriting, " Life of Alleyn," p. 53.   Also as Wotton's in
MS. Malone, 13, fol. 11 ; in MS. Malone, 19, p. 138 ; and
in Clark's " Aurea Legenda," 1682, p. 96.   There are
many other old copies.   Said to be almost identical with a
German poem of the same age ; " Notes and Queries," vol.
ix., p. 420.

IV.

THIS HYMN

WAS MADE BY SIR H. WOTTON, WHEN HE WAS
AN AMBASSADOR AT VENICE, IN THE
TIME OF A GREAT SICK-
NESS THERE.[1]

ETERNAL mover, whose diffused glory,
　　To show our grovelling reason what
　　　　Thou art,
　　Unfolds itself in clouds of nature's story,
Where man, thy proudest creature, acts his part,
Whom yet, alas, I know not why, we call
The world's contracted sum, the little all;

For what are we but lumps of walking clay?
　　Why should we swell? whence should our spirits
　　　　rise?
Are not brute beasts as strong, and birds as gay,—
　　Trees longer lived, and creeping things as wise?
Only our souls were left an inward light,
To feel our weakness, and confess Thy might.

Thou then, our strength, Father of life and death,
　　To whom our thanks, our vows, ourselves we owe,

---

[1] "Rel. Wotton." Erroneously ascribed to Sir Walter
Raleigh, as written "in the unquiet rest of his *last sick-
ness,*" in "Topographer," vol. i. p. 425, on the authority of
a Brit. Mus. MS.

From me, Thy tenant of this fading breath,
    Accept those lines which from Thy goodness flow,
And Thou, that wert Thy regal Prophet's muse,
Do not Thy praise in weaker strains refuse!

Let these poor notes ascend unto Thy throne,
    Where majesty doth sit with mercy crowned,
Where my Redeemer lives, in whom alone
    The errors of my wandering life are drowned:
Where all the choir of Heaven resound the same.
That only Thine, Thine is the saving name!

Well, then, my soul, joy in the midst of pain:
    Thy Christ, that conquered Hell, shall from above
With greater triumph yet return again,
    And conquer His own justice with His love;
Commanding earth and seas to render those
Unto His bliss, for whom He paid His woes.

Now have I done; now are my thoughts at peace;
    And now my joys are stronger than my grief:
I feel those comforts, that shall never cease,
    Future in hope, but present in belief:
Thy words are true, Thy promises are just,
And Thou wilt find Thy dearly-bought in dust!

                                H. WOTTON.

V.

UPON THE SUDDEN RESTRAINT OF
THE EARL OF SOMERSET

THEN FALLING FROM FAVOUR.[1]

(Oct. 18, 1615.)

AZZLED thus with height of place,
    Whilst our hopes our wits beguile
No man marks the narrow space
    'Twixt a prison and a smile.

Then, since Fortune's favours fade,
    You, that in her arms do sleep,
Learn to swim, and not to wade;
    For the hearts of kings are deep.

But if greatness be so blind
    As to trust in towers of air,
Let it be with goodness lined,
    That at least the fall be fair.

Then, though darkened, you shall say,
    When friends fail and princes frown,
Virtue is the roughest way,
    But proves at night a bed of down.

H. W.

[1] " Rel. Wotton." Also as Wotton's in Sancroft's MS., Tann.
465, fol. 61 *verso;* in MS. Rawl. Poet. 147, p. 97, with the
erased title, " Sr H. W. on ye Duke of Somer. ;" and in
Clark's " Aurea Legenda," 1682, p. 97. In some less
authorized copies it is represented as addressed "to the
Lord Bacon, when falling from favour." See Park's Wal-
pole, " R. and N. A.," vol. ii. p. 208, note; and "Notes and
Queries," vol. i. p. 302.

VI.

TO A NOBLE FRIEND IN HIS SICKNESS.[1]

NTIMELY fever, rude insulting guest,
   How didst thou with such unharmo-
      nious heat
Dare to distune his well-composed rest
Whose heart so just and noble strokes did beat?

What if his youth and spirits well may bear
   More thick assaults and stronger siege than this?
We measure not his courage, but our fear :
   Not what ourselves, but what the times may miss.

Had not that blood, which thrice his veins did yield,
   Been better treasured for some glorious day,
At farthest West to paint the liquid field,
   And with new worlds his Master's love to pay?

But let those thoughts, sweet Lord, repose awhile ;
   Tend only now thy vigour to regain ;
And pardon these poor rhymes, that would beguile,
   With mine own grief, some portion of thy pain.

                        H. W.

---

[1] " Rel. Wotton." In MS. Rawl. Poet. 147, p. 101, it is
entitled "On the Duke of Buckingham sick of a fever;" and
has the signature " Sr. Henry Wotton."

VII.

ON HIS MISTRESS, THE QUEEN OF BOHEMIA.[1]

(Circ. 1620.)

YOU meaner beauties of the night,
　　That poorly satisfy our eyes
More by your number than your light,
　　You common people of the skies ;
What are you when the moon shall rise ?

You curious chanters of the wood,
　　That warble forth Dame Nature's lays,
Thinking your passions understood
　　By your weak accents ; what's your praise,
When Philomel her voice shall raise ?

You violets that first appear,
　　By your pure purple mantles known
Like the proud virgins of the year,
　　As if the spring were all your own ;
What are you when the rose is blown ?

---

[1] " Rel. Wotton." It was printed with music as early as
1624, in Est's " Sixth Set of Books," &c., and is found in
many MSS., *e.g.* MS. Tann. 465, fol. 43, and MS. Malone
19, p. 23, title, " To the Spanish Lady ;" *i e.* the Infanta.
Found also anonymously in " Wit's Recreations," 1640, and
in " Wit's Interpreter," 1671, p. 267, and with a second
part in " Cantus, Songs and Fancies," &c., Aberdeen, 1682
(third edition), No. LIV. There are additional verses in
several of these copies.

So, when my mistress shall be seen
　In form and beauty of her mind,
By virtue first, then choice, a Queen,
　Tell me if she were not designed
　The eclipse and glory of her kind?
H. W.

VIII.

TEARS AT THE GRAVE OF SIR ALBERTUS MORTON,

WHO WAS BURIED AT SOUTHAMPTON:

WEPT BY SIR H. WOTTON.[1]

(Died Nov. 1625.)

 ILENCE in truth would speak my sorrow
　　　　　best,
　　　For deepest wounds can least their
　　　　feelings tell;
Yet let me borrow from mine own unrest
　But time to bid him, whom I loved, farewell.

O my unhappy lines! you that before
　Have served my youth to vent some wanton cries,
And now, congealed with grief, can scarce implore
　Strength to accent,—Here my Albertus lies!

---

[1] "Rel. Wotton." and Walton's "Life of Wotton." Also
in MS. Rawl. Poet. 147, p. 107.

This is the sable stone,—this is the cave
    And womb of earth that doth his corpse embrace ;
While others sing his praise, let me engrave
    These bleeding numbers to adorn the place.

Here will I paint the characters of woe ;
    Here will I pay my tribute to the dead ;
And here my faithful tears in showers shall flow,
    To humanize the flints whereon I tread :

Where, though I mourn my matchless loss alone,
    And none between my weakness judge and me,
Yet even these gentle walls allow my moan,
    Whose doleful echoes to my plaints agree.

But is he gone ? and live I rhyming here,
    As if some Muse would listen to my lay,
When all distuned sit wailing for their dear,
    And bathe the banks where he was wont to play ?

Dwell thou in endless light, discharged soul,
    Freed now from Nature's and from Fortune's trust !
While on this fluent globe my glass shall roll,
    And run the rest of my remaining dust.

                       H. WOTTON.

IX.

UPON THE DEATH OF SIR ALBERT.
MORTON'S WIFE.[1]

E first deceased; she for a little tried
To live without him, liked it not, and
died.

H. WOTTON.

X.

A SHORT HYMN UPON THE BIRTH OF
PRINCE CHARLES.[2]

(May 29, 1630.)

OU that on stars do look,
 Arrest not there your sight,
Though Nature's fairest book,
 And signed with propitious light;
Our blessing now is more divine
Than planets that at noon did shine.

---

[1] " Rel. Wotton."   Also in Picke's " Festum Voluptatis,"
1639; and, with a different title, in Philipot's edit. of Cam-
den's " Remains," 1657, p. 406.   And also in Fuller,
" Worthies of Essex," p. 340.
 [2] " Rel. Wotton."

To Thee alone be praise,
    From whom our joy descends,
Thou cheerer of our days,
    Of causes first, and last of ends :
To Thee this May we sing, by whom
Our roses from the lilies bloom.

Upon this royal flower,
    Sprung from the chastest bed,
Thy glorious sweetness shower ;
    And first let myrtles crown his head,
Then palms and laurels wreathed between :
But let the cypress late be seen.

And so succeeding men,
    When they the fulness see
Of this our joy, shall then
    In consort join, as well as we,
To celebrate His praise above
That spreads our land with fruits of love.
                    H. WOTTON.

XI.

AN ODE TO THE KING,

AT HIS RETURNING FROM SCOTLAND TO THE
QUEEN AFTER HIS CORONATION THERE.[1]

(1633.)

ROUSE up thyself, my gentle Muse,
    Though now our green conceits be
        grey,
And yet once more do not refuse

[1] "Rel. Wotton." Transcribed as Wotton's in MS. Tann.

To take thy Phrygian harp, and play
In honour of this cheerful day.

Make first a song of joy and love,
　　Which chastely flame in royal eyes;
Then tune it to the spheres above
　　When the benignest stars do rise,
　　And sweet conjunctions grace the skies.

To this let all good hearts resound,
　　While diadems invest his head;
Long may he live, whose life doth bound
　　More than his laws, and better lead
　　By high example than by dread!

Long may he round about him see
　　His roses and his lilies blown;
Long may his only dear and he
　　Joy in ideas of their own,
　　And kingdom's hopes so timely sown;

Long may they both contend to prove,
That best of crowns is such a love!

H. W.

465, fol. 61, *verso*, and MS. Rawl. Poet. 147, p. 96. Erroneously inserted among Ben Jonson's "Works," vol. ix. p. 52, edit. Gifford.

XII.

ON A BANK AS I SAT A-FISHING.

A DESCRIPTION OF THE SPRING.[1]

(*Circ.* 1638.)

AND now all nature seemed in love;
The lusty sap began to move;
New juice did stir the embracing vines,
And birds had drawn their valentines;
The jealous trout, that low did lie,
Rose at a well-dissembled fly:
There stood my friend, with patient skill,
Attending of his trembling quill.
Already were the eaves possessed
With the swift pilgrim's daubed nest:
The groves already did rejoice
In Philomel's triumphing voice.
The showers were short, the weather mild,
The morning fresh, the evening smiled.
Joan takes her neat-rubbed pail, and now
She trips to milk the sand-red cow;
Where, for some sturdy football swain,
Joan strokes a sillabub or twain.
The fields and gardens were beset
With tulip, crocus, violet;

---

[1] "Rel. Wotton." Also as Wotton's in MS. Tann. 465, fol. 61, *verso*; in MS. Rawl. Poet. 147, p. 47; and in Walton's "Complete Angler," p. 78, edit. Nicolas, where it is said to have been written when Wotton was "beyond seventy years of age." He was born in 1568.

And now, though late, the modest rose
Did more than half a blush disclose.
Thus all look'd gay, all full of cheer,
To welcome the new liveried year.

H. W.

XIII.

A TRANSLATION OF THE CIV. PSALM

TO THE ORIGINAL SENSE.[1]

Y soul, exalt the Lord with hymns of
    praise:
    O Lord, my God, how boundless is
    Thy might!
Whose Throne of State is clothed with glorious rays,
    And round about hast robed Thyself with light;
Who like a curtain hast the heavens displayed,
And in the watery roofs Thy chambers laid:

Whose chariots are the thickened clouds above;
    Who walk'st upon the winged winds below;
At whose command the airy spirits move,
    And fiery meteors their obedience show;
Who on his base the earth did'st firmly found,
And mad'st the deep to circumvest it round.

The waves that rise would drown the highest hill,
    But at Thy check they fly, and when they hear
Thy thundering voice, they post to do Thy Will,
    And bound their furies in their proper sphere,

[1] "Rel. Wotton."

Where surging floods and valing ebbs can tell,
That none beyond Thy marks must sink or swell.

Who hath disposed, but Thou, the winding way,
  Where springs down from the steepy crags do
    beat,
At which both fostered beasts their thirsts allay,
  And the wild asses come to quench their heat;
Where birds resort, and, in their kind, Thy praise
Among the branches chant in warbling lays?

The mounts are watered from Thy dwelling-place;
  The barns and meads are filled for man and beast;
Wine glads the heart, and oil adorns the face,
  And bread, the staff whereon our strength doth
    rest;
Nor shrubs alone feel Thy sufficing hand,
But even the cedars that so proudly stand.

So have the fowls their sundry seats to breed;
  The ranging stork in stately beeches dwells;
The climbing goats on hills securely feed;
  The mining conies shroud in rocky cells:
Nor can the heavenly lights their course forget,
The moon her turns, or sun his times to set.

Thou mak'st the night to overveil the day:
  Then savage beasts creep from the silent wood;
Then lions' whelps lie roaring for their prey,
  And at Thy powerful hand demand their food;
Who when at morn they all recouch again,
Then toiling man till eve pursues his pain.

O Lord! when on Thy various works we look,
  How richly furnished is the earth we tread!

Where, in the fair contents of Nature's book,
  We may the wonders of Thy wisdom read :—
Nor earth alone, but lo ! the sea so wide,
Where great and small, a world of creatures glide :

There go the ships that furrow out their way ;
  Yea, there of whales enormous sights we see,
Which yet have scope among the rest to play,
  And all do wait for their support on Thee ;
Who hast assigned each thing his proper food,
And in due season dost dispense Thy good.

They gather when Thy gifts Thou dost divide ;
  Their stores abound, if Thou Thy hand enlarge,
Confused they are when Thou Thy beams dost hide ;
  In dust resolved if Thou their breath discharge ;
Again, when Thou of life renew'st the seeds,
The withered fields revest their cheerful weeds.

Be ever gloried here Thy sovereign name,
  That Thou may'st smile on all which Thou hast
      made ;
Whose frown alone can shake this earthly frame,
  And at whose touch the hills in smoke shall vade !
For me, may, while I breathe, both harp and voice
In sweet indictment of Thy hymns rejoice !

Let sinners fail, let all profaneness cease :—
His praise, my soul, His praise shall be thy peace.
                              H. WOTTON.

XIV.

A HYMN TO MY GOD,

IN A NIGHT OF MY LATE SICKNESS.[1]

(1638 or 1639.)

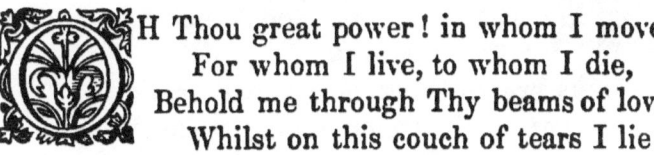H Thou great power! in whom I move,
 For whom I live, to whom I die,
Behold me through Thy beams of love.
 Whilst on this couch of tears I lie;
And cleanse my sordid soul within
By Thy Christ's blood, the bath of sin !

No hallowed oils, no grains I need,
 No rags of saints, no purging fire ;
One rosy drop from David's seed
 Was worlds of seas to quench Thine ire.
O precious ransom ! which once paid,
That *consummatum est* was said :

And said by Him that said no more,
 But sealed it with His sacred breath :
Thou, then, that hast dispunged my score,
 And dying wast the death of Death,
Be to me now, on Thee I call,
My life, my strength, my joy, my all!

       H. WOTTON.

[1] "Rel. Wotton." among the letters. There are copies in MS. Tann. 465, p. 137; MS. Rawl. Poet. 147, p. 101; MS. Ashm. 38, No. 172, &c.; and in Clark's "Aurea Legenda," 1682, p. 141.

XV.

TO THE RARELY ACCOMPLISHED, AND WORTHY
OF BEST EMPLOYMENT, MASTER HOWELL,
UPON HIS VOCAL FOREST.[1]

ELIEVE it, Sir, you happily have hit
Upon a curious fancy, of such wit,
That far transcends the vulgar ; for
each line
Methinks breathes Barclay, or a Boccaline.
I know you might (none better) make the vine,
The olive, ivy, mulberry, and pine,
With others, their own dialects expose,
But you have taught them all rich English prose.
I end and envy ; but must justly say,
Who makes trees speak so well, deserves *the bay*.

HENRY WOTTON.

XVI.

A DESCRIPTION OF THE COUNTRY'S
RECREATIONS.[2]

(Author uncertain.)

UIVERING fears, heart-tearing cares,
Anxious sighs, untimely tears,
Fly, fly to courts !
Fly to fond worldlings' sports,

---

[1] Prefixed to Howell's "Dodona's Grove," 1640. No
doubt the book was submitted in MS. to Wotton, who died
in 1639.

[2] " Rel. Wotton." signed as below. Also in Walton's

Where strained sardonic smiles are glozing still,
And grief is forced to laugh against her will ;
  Where mirth's but mummery,
  And sorrows only real be ! ·

Fly from our country pastimes ! fly,
Sad troop of human misery !
  Come, serene looks,
  Clear as the crystal brooks,
Or the pure azured heaven, that smiles to see
The rich attendance of our poverty !
  Peace, and a secure mind,
  Which all men seek, we only find.

Abused mortals ! did you know
Where joy, heart's ease, and comforts grow,
  You'd scorn proud towers,
  And seek them in these bowers,
Where winds sometimes our woods perhaps may
   shake,
But blustering care could never tempest make,
  Nor murmurs e'er come nigh us,
  Saving of fountains that glide by us.

Here's no fantastic mask, nor dance
But of our kids, that frisk and prance :
  Nor wars are seen,
  Unless upon the green

"Complete Angler," p. 309, edit. Nicolas, as "doubtless
made either by (Sir H. Wotton) or by a lover of angling." An
anonymous copy in "Tixall Poetry," p. 297, as "Rusticatio
Religiosi in Vacantiis." Claimed without authority for Sir
W. Raleigh by Brydges and the Oxford editors.

Two harmless lambs are butting one the other;
Which done, both bleating run, each to his mother:
    And wounds are never found,
    Save what the ploughshare gives the ground.

Here are no false entrapping baits,
To hasten too-too hasty Fates;
    Unless it be
    The fond credulity
Of silly fish, which, worldling-like, still look
Upon the bait, but never on the hook:
    Nor envy, unless among
    The birds, for prize of their sweet song.

Go! let the diving negro seek
For gems hid in some forlorn creek;
    We all pearls scorn,
    Save what the dewy morn
Congeals upon each little spire of grass,
Which careless shepherds beat down as they pass;
    And gold ne'er here appears,
    Save what the yellow Ceres bears.

Blest, silent groves!   O may ye be
For ever mirth's best nursery!
    May pure contents
    For ever pitch their tents
Upon these downs, these meads, these rocks, these
    mountains,
And peace still slumber by these purling fountains!
    Which we may every year
    Find when we come a-fishing here.

                    IGNOTO.

XVII.

A FAREWELL TO THE VANITIES
OF THE WORLD.[1]

(Author uncertain.)

FAREWELL, ye gilded follies, pleasing
    troubles !
Farewell, ye honoured rags, ye glorious
    bubbles !
Fame's but a hollow echo ; gold pure clay ;
Honour the darling but of one short day ;
Beauty, the eyes' idol, but a damasked skin ;
State but a golden prison to live in,
And torture free-born minds ; embroidered trains
Merely but pageants for proud swelling veins ;
And blood allied to greatness is alone
Inherited, not purchased, nor our own :
Fame, honour, beauty, state, train, blood, and birth,
Are but the fading blossoms of the earth.

[1] Walton's "Complete Angler," p. 311, edit. Nicolas ; in
the first two editions as "some say written by Dr. D.," but
afterwards as "some say written by Sir Harry Wotton."
In MS. Ashm. 38 it is entitled "Doctor Donn's Valediction
to the world." In "Wit's Interpreter," 1671, p. 269, it is
ascribed to Sir Kenelm Digby. Sir H. Nicolas, without
any authority that I know of, says that "these verses are
also said to have been written by Sir W. Raleigh, when a
prisoner in the Tower, shortly before his execution." Arch-
bishop Sancroft gives them anonymously with the title,
"An hermit in an arbour, with a prayer-book in his hand,
his foot spurning a globe, thus speaketh ;" MS. Tann. 465,
fol. 59.

I would be great, but that the sun doth still
Level his rays against the rising hill;
I would be high, but see the proudest oak
Most subject to the rending thunder-stroke;
I would be rich, but see men too unkind
Dig in the bowels of the richest mind;
I would be wise, but that I often see
The fox suspected, whilst the ass goes free;
I would be fair, but see the fair and proud,
Like the bright sun, oft setting in a cloud;
I would be poor, but know the humble grass
Still trampled on by each unworthy ass:
Rich, hated; wise, suspected; scorned, if poor;
Great, feared; fair, tempted; high, still envied
　　　　more:
I have wished all, but now I wish for neither,
Great, high, rich, wise, nor fair; poor I'll be rather.

Would the world now adopt me for her heir;
Would Beauty's queen entitle me the fair;
Fame speak me Fortune's minion; could I vie
Angels with India; with a speaking eye
Command bare heads, bowed knees, strike Justice
　　　　dumb,
As well as blind and lame; or give a tongue
To stones by epitaphs; be called great master
In the loose rhymes of every poetaster;
Could I be more than any man that lives,
Great, fair, rich, wise, all in superlatives;
Yet I more freely would these gifts resign,
Than ever Fortune would have made them mine;
And hold one minute of this holy leisure
Beyond the riches of this empty pleasure.

Welcome, pure thoughts! welcome, ye silent groves!
These guests, these courts, my soul most dearly
      loves:
Now the winged people of the sky shall sing
My cheerful anthems to the gladsome spring;
A Prayer-book now shall be my looking-glass,
In which I will adore sweet Virtue's face.
Here dwell no hateful looks, no palace-cares,
No broken vows dwell here, nor pale-faced fears;
Then here I'll sit and sigh my hot love's folly,
And learn to affect an holy melancholy;
And if contentment be a stranger then,
I'll ne'er look for it, but in heaven, again.

XVIII.

IMITATIO HORATIANÆ ODES IX.

"DONEC GRATUS ERAM TIBI."—LIB. III.

A DIALOGUE BETWIXT GOD AND THE SOUL.[1]

(Author unknown.)

Soul.

WHILST my soul's eye beheld no light,
    But what streamed from Thy gracious
       sight,
To me the world's greatest King
Seemed but some little vulgar thing.

[1] "Rel. Wotton."   Claimed without authority for Sir W.
Raleigh by Brydges.

God. Whilst thou proved'st pure, and that in thee
    I could glass all my Deity;
    How glad did I from heaven depart,
    To find a lodging in thy heart!

Soul. Now fame and greatness bear the sway;
    'Tis they that hold my prison's key:
    For whom my soul would die, might she
    Leave them her immortality.

God. I and some few pure souls conspire,
    And burn both in a mutual fire,
    For whom I'ld die once more, ere they
    Should miss of heaven's eternal day.

Soul. But, Lord, what if I turn again,
    And, with an adamantine chain,
    Lock me to Thee?   What if I chase
    The world away to give Thee place?

God. Then, though these souls, in whom I joy,
    Are seraphims,—thou but a toy,
    A foolish toy,—yet once more I
    Would with thee live, and for thee die.

                                    IGNOTO.

XIX.

DOCTOR BROOKE OF TEARS.[1]

WHO would have thought there could have
        been
    Such joy in tears wept for our sin?
    Mine eyes have seen, my heart hath
        proved,

[1] "Rel. Wotton." as "Doctor B. of Tears." The full
name was obtained from a MS. belonging to Mr. J. P.

The most and best of earthly joys;
    The sweets of love, and being loved;
Masks, feasts and plays, and such like toys:
    Yet this one tear, which now doth fall,
    In true delight exceeds them all.

Indeed mine eyes at first let in
Those guests that did these woes begin;
    Therefore mine eyes in tears and grief
Are justly drowned; but that those tears
    Should comfort bring, is past belief.
O God! in this Thy grace appears,
    Thou that mak'st light from darkness spring,
    Mak'st joys to weep, and sorrows sing.

O where am I? what may I think?
Help, help! alas, my heart doth sink!
    Thus lost in seas of woe,
Thus laden with my sin,
Waves of despair dash in,
    And threat my overthrow.
What heart oppressed with such a weight
Can choose but break, and perish quite?

Yet, as at sea in storms, men use,
The ship to save, their goods to lose;
    So in this fearful storm
This danger to prevent,
Before all hope be spent,
    I'll choose the lesser harm:
My tears to seas I will convert,
And drown my eyes to save my heart.

Collier. Erroneously included in the " Poems of Pembroke
and Rudyard," 1660, p. 46, with the title, " Benj. Rudier
of Tears."

                        ɪ

O God, my God! what shall I give
To Thee in thanks?   I am and live
  In Thee, and Thou didst safe preserve
My health, my fame, my goods, my rent;
  Thou mak'st me eat while others starve,
And sing, whilst others do lament.
  Such unto me Thy blessings are,
  As if I were Thy only care.

But, O my God! Thou art more kind,
When I look inward on my mind:
  Thou fill'st my heart with humble joy,
With patience, meekness, fervent love,
  Which doth all other loves destroy,
With faith, which nothing can remove,
  And hope assured of heaven's bliss:—
  This is my state, Thy grace is this.

XX.

I.

BY CHIDICK TYCHBORN,

**BEING YOUNG AND THEN IN THE TOWER, THE
NIGHT BEFORE HIS EXECUTION.[1]**

(1586.)

MY prime of youth is but a frost of cares;
    My feast of joy is but a dish of
        pain;
    My crop of corn is but a field of tares;
And all my good is but vain hope of gain;

[1] " Rel. Wotton." and in numerous MS. copies; e. g. Harl.
MS. 6910, fol. 141, verso; MS. Ashm. 781, p. 138; MS.
Malone, 19, p. 44, &c.

The day is fled, and yet I saw no sun;
And now I live, and now my life is done!

The spring is past, and yet it hath not sprung;
   The fruit is dead, and yet the leaves are green;
My youth is gone, and yet I am but young;
   I saw the world, and yet I was not seen;
My thread is cut, and yet it is not spun;
And now I live, and now my life is done!

I sought my death, and found it in my womb;
   I looked for life, and saw it was a shade;
I trod the earth, and knew it was my tomb;
   And now I die, and now I am but made;
The glass is full, and now my glass is run;
And now I live, and now my life is done!

II.

AN ANSWER TO MR. TICHBORNE,

WHO WAS EXECUTED WITH BABINGTON.[1]

THY flower of youth is with a north wind
      blasted;
      Thy feast of joy is an idea found;
      Thy corn is shed, thy untimely harvest
   wasted;
Thy good in ill, thy hope in hurt [is drowned];
Dark was thy day, and shadow was thy sun,
And, by such lights, thy life untimely spun.

[1] From a MS. belonging to Mr. J. P. Collier.

Thy tale was nought, thy oratory told;
  Thy fruit is rotten, and thy leaves are gone;
Thyself wert young in years, in time grown old;
  The world accounts thee not worth thinking on;
Thy thread [of life]'s not cut nor spun, but broken;
So let thy heart, though yet it be but open.

Thou sought'st thy death, and found'st it in desert;
  Thou look'dst for life, yet lewdly felt it fade;
Thou trodd'st on earth, and now in earth thou art;
  And men may wish that thou hadst ne'er been
      [made];
Thy glory and thy glass are timeless run,
Which, O unhappy! by thyself was done.

XXI.

RISE, O MY SOUL.[1]

(Author unknown.)

RISE, O my soul! with thy desires to
    heaven,
  And with divinest contemplation use
  Thy time, where time's eternity is given,
And let vain thoughts no more thy thoughts abuse:
But down in [midnight] darkness let them lie;
So live thy better, let thy worse thoughts die!

And thou, my soul, inspired with holy flame,
  View and review, with most regardful eye,

[1] "Rel. Wotton." Claimed without authority for Raleigh by Brydges and the Oxford editors.

That holy cross, whence thy salvation came,
On which thy Saviour and thy sin did die!
For in that sacred object is much pleasure,
And in that Saviour is my life, my treasure.

To thee, O Jesu! I direct my eyes;
To Thee my hands, to Thee my humble knees;
To Thee my heart shall offer sacrifice;
To Thee my thoughts, who my thoughts only sees:
To Thee myself,—myself and all I give;
To Thee I die; to Thee I only live!

IGNOTO.

XXII.

THE WORLD.[1]

(By Lord Bacon.)

THE world's a bubble, and the life of man
Less than a span;
In his conception wretched, from the
womb,
So to the tomb;

[1] " Rel. Wotton." Signed as below in all editions after the first, where it is marked " Ignoto." Ascribed to Lord Bacon in Farnaby's " Florilegium," 1629, p. 10. Compare Spedding's edit. of Bacon's " Works," vol. vii. p. 269. In MS. Rawl. Poet. 117, fol. 161, it was first entitled "The Bubble, by R. W.;" (? H. W.) altered to "by ye Lord Bacon." In MS. Ashm. 38, p. 2, the first title was, " On Man's Mortality, by Doctor Donn;" altered to " Sr Fran. Bacon." In a MS. belonging to the late Mr. Pickering the title is, " Upon the Misery of Man;" the first signature is " Henry Harrington," altered to " Ld Verulam Viscount St. Alban's."

Curst from his cradle, and brought up to years
    With cares and fears.
Who then to frail mortality shall trust
But limns on water, or but writes in dust.

Yet, whilst with sorrow here we live oppressed,
    What life is best?
Courts are but only superficial schools,
    To dandle fools;
The rural part is turned into a den
    Of savage men;
And where's a city from foul vice so free
But may be termed the worst of all the three?

Domestic cares afflict the husband's bed,
    Or pains his head:
Those that live single take it for a curse,
    Or do things worse:
These would have children; those that have
    them moan,
    Or wish them gone,
What is it, then, to have or have no wife,
But single thraldom or a double strife?

Our own affections still at home to please
    Is a disease;
To cross the seas to any foreign soil,
    Peril and toil;
Wars with their noise affright us; when they cease,
    We're worse in peace:
What then remains, but that we still should cry
For being born, and, being born, to die?

                    FRA. LORD BACON.

XXIII.

VERSES MADE BY MR. FRA. BACON.[1]

THE man of life upright, whose guiltless
    heart is free
    From all dishonest deeds, and thoughts
      of vanity;
That man whose silent days in harmless joys are
    spent,
Whom hopes cannot delude, nor fortune discontent;
That man needs neither tower nor armour for
    defence,
Nor secret vaults to fly from thunder's violence.
He only can behold with unaffrighted eyes
The horrors of the deep and terrors of the skies.
Thus, scorning all the care that fate or fortune
    brings,
He makes the heaven his book, his wisdom heavenly
    things,
Good thoughts his only friends, his wealth a well-
    spent age;
The earth his sober inn,—a quiet pilgrimage.

                        FRA. BACON.

[1] Printed from a Brit. Mus. MS. by Park, " Walpole's
Royal and Noble Authors," vol. ii. p. 217, and Spedding,
" Bacon's Works," vol. vii. p. 269. I have corrected one
or two words from an anonymous copy in Chetham MS.
8012, p. 79, which, however, omits lines 7 and 8.

XXIV.

I.

DE MORTE.[1]

(Author unknown.)

MAN'S life's a tragedy: his mother's womb,
From which he enters, is the tiring room;
This spacious earth the theatre; and the
    stage
That country which he lives in : passions, rage.
Folly, and vice are actors ; the first cry,
The prologue to the ensuing tragedy ;
The former act consisteth of dumb shows ;
The second, he to more perfection grows ;
I' the third he is a man, and doth begin
To nurture vice, and act the deeds of sin ;
I' the fourth, declines ; I' the fifth, diseases clog
And trouble him ; then death's his epilogue.

IGNOTO.

II.

EPIGRAM.[2]

(Author unknown.)

F breath were made for every man to
    buy,
The poor man could not live,—rich
    would not die.

---

[1] " Rel. Wotton." Claimed without authority for Raleigh
by Brydges and the Oxford editors.
[2] " Rel. Wotton."

XXV.

SPECIMENS OF EPIGRAMS BY JOHN HOSKINS.

I. JOHN HOSKINS TO HIS LITTLE CHILD BENJAMIN, FROM THE TOWER.[1]

WEET Benjamin, since thou art young.
And hast not yet the use of tongue,
Make it thy slave, while thou art free;
Imprison it, lest it do thee.

Ad Filiolum suum Benjamin.[2]

Dum puer es, vanæ nescisque incommoda vocis,
Vincula da linguæ, vel tibi lingua dabit.

II. VERSES PRESENTED TO THE KING BY MRS. HOSKINS, IN THE BEHALF OF HER HUSBAND, PRISONER.[3]

HE worst is told; the best is hid:
Kings know not all; I would they did:
What though my husband once have
erred?
Men more to blame have been preferred.

[1] "Rel. Wotton." edit. 1672. Often found in MSS. with the Latin version here appended.
[2] MS. Malone 19, p. 141; Mr. Pickering's MS. fol. 151, &c.
[3] MS. Malone 16, p. 20; in other MSS. in a longer form.

Who hath not erred, he doth not live;
He erred but once; once, king, forgive!

III. OF THE LOSS OF TIME.[1]

IF life be time that here is lent,
    And time on earth be cast away,
Whoso his time hath here misspent,
    Hath hastened his own dying day:
So it doth prove a killing crime
To massacre our living time.

If doing nought be like to death,
    Of him that doth, chameleon-wise,
Take only pains to draw his breath,
    The passers-by may pasquilize,
    Not, here he lives; but, here he dies.

IV. AN EPITAPH ON A MAN FOR DOING NOTHING.[2]

HERE lies the man was born and cried,
Told threescore years, fell sick, and died.

[1] Chetham MS. 8012, p. 76.
[2] Chetham MS. 8012, p. 158; also in Philipot's edit. of
Camden's "Remains," 1657, p. 399.

PART III.

SPECIMENS OF

OTHER COURTLY POETS

FROM 1540 TO 1650.

SPECIMENS OF

OTHER COURTLY POETS.

I.

THE LOVER COMPLAINETH THE UNKINDNESS OF HIS LOVE.[1]

(By Sir Thomas Wyatt or Viscount Rochford. Before 1542.)

MY lute, awake ! perform the last
    Labour that thou and I shall waste,
      And end that I have now begun ;
    And when this song is sung and past,
My lute, be still ! for I have done.

As to be heard where ear is none ;
As lead to grave in marble stone ;
    My song may pierce her heart as soon :
Should we then sigh, or sing, or moan ?
    No, no, my lute, for I have done.

[1] In Tottel's " Songs and Sonnets," 1557, and in Nott's " Wyatt," p. 20, as Sir Thomas Wyatt's. Ascribed to Rochford in " Nugæ Antiquæ," vol. ii. p. 400, edit. Park.

The rocks do not so cruelly
Repulse the waves continually
　　As she my suit and affection:
So that I am past remedy:
　　Whereby my lute and I have done.

Proud of the spoil that thou hast got
Of simple hearts, thorough Love's shot,
　　By whom, unkind, thou hast them won;
Think not he hath his bow forgot,
　　Although my lute and I have done.

Vengeance shall fall on thy disdain:
Thou mak'st but game on earnest pain:
　　Think not alone under the sun
Unquit to cause thy lovers plain,
　　Although my lute and I have done.

May chance thee lie, withered and old,
In winter nights that are so cold,
　　Plaining in vain unto the moon.
Thy wishes then dare not be told;
　　Care then who list, for I have done.

And then may chance thee to repent
The time that thou hast lost and spent,
　　To cause thy lovers sigh and swoon:
Then shalt thou know beauty but lent,
　　And wish and want as I have done.

Now cease, my lute! This is the last
Labour that thou and I shall waste,
　　And ended is that we begun:
Now is this song both sung and past:
　　My lute, be still! for I have done.

II.

A DESCRIPTION OF A MOST NOBLE LADY.[1]

(Uncertain, but claimed for John Heywood.)
(Before 1557.)

IVE place, you ladies, and begone!
 Boast not yourselves at all!
For here at hand approacheth one
 Whose face will stain you all.

The virtue of her lively looks
 Excels the precious stone;
I wish to have none other books
 To read or look upon.

In each of her two crystal eyes
 Smileth a naked boy;
It would you all in heart suffice
 To see that lamp of joy.

I think Nature hath lost the mould
 Where she her shape did take;
Or else I doubt if Nature could
 So fair a creature make.

[1] In Tottel's "Songs and Sonnets," 1557, as "A Praise of his Lady," among "Uncertain Authors." Ascribed to John Heywood by W. Forrest (or the transcriber of his poems), in a copy containing many alterations, and adapting the poem to Queen Mary, in Harl. MS. 1703, fol. 108; title as above.

She may be well compared
　　Unto the Phœnix kind,
Whose like was never seen nor heard,
　　That any man can find.

In life she is Diana chaste,
　　In truth Penelope;
In work and eke in deed steadfast.
　　What will you more we say?

If all the world were sought so far,
　　Who could find such a wight?
Her beauty twinkleth like a star
　　Within the frosty night.

Her roseal colour comes and goes
　　With such a comely grace,
More ruddier, too, than doth the rose,
　　Within her lively face.

At Bacchus' feast none shall her meet,
　　Ne at no wanton play,
Nor gazing in an open street,
　　Nor gadding as a stray.

The modest mirth that she doth use
　　Is mixed with shamefastness;
All vice she doth wholly refuse,
　　And hateth idleness.

O Lord! it is a world to see
　　How virtue can repair,
And deck her in such honesty,
　　Whom nature made so fair.

Truly she doth so far exceed
　　Our women nowadays,

As doth the gillyflower a weed ;
  And more a thousand ways.

How might I do to get a graff
  Of this unspotted tree?
For all the rest are plain but chaff,
  Which seem good corn to be.

This gift alone I shall her give:
  When death doth what he can,
Her honest fame shall ever live
  Within the mouth of man.

III.

BEING DISDAINED HE COMPLAINETH.[1]

(By Thomas Lord Vaux.   Died in 1557.)

F friendless faith, if guiltless thought
    may shield ;
    If simple truth that never meant to
    swerve ;
If dear desire accepted fruit do yield ;
  If greedy lust in loyal life do serve ;
Then may my plaint bewail my heavy harm,
That, seeking calm, have stumbled on the storm.

My wonted cheer,—eclipsed by the cloud
  Of deep disdain, through error of report,
If weary woe enwrapped in the shroud,—
  Lies slain by tongue of the unfriendly sort ;

[1] " Paradise of Dainty Devices," 1576, &c.

K

Yet heaven and earth, and all that nature wrought,
I call to vow of my unspotted thought.

No shade I seek in part to shield my taint,
   But simple truth; I hunt no other suit:
On that I ga[g]e the issue of my plaint;
   If that I quail, let justice me confute:
If that my place among the guiltless sort
Repay by doom my name and good report.

Go, heavy verse; pursue desired grace;
   Where pity shrined in cell of secret breast
Awaits my haste the rightful lot to place,
   And loathes to see the guiltless man oppressed:
Whose virtues great have crowned her more with
     fame
Than kingly state, though largely shine the same.

L. VAUX.

IV.

OF THE MEAN ESTATE.[1]

(By Thomas Lord Vaux or W. Hunnis.)

THE higher that the cedar tree unto the
     heavens do[th] grow,
   The more in danger is the top when
     sturdy winds gan blow.
Who judges them in princely throne to be devoid
   of hate,

---

[1] " Paradise of Dainty Devices;" in edit. 1578 signed W.
H; in edits. 1580 and 1596 signed W. Hunnis; in other
edits. L. V. (or Lord Vaux).

Doth not yet know what heaps of ill lie hid in such
    estate.
Such dangers great, such gripes of mind, such toil
    do they sustain,
That oftentimes of God they wish to be unkinged
    again.

For as the huge and mighty rocks withstand the
    raging seas,
So kingdoms in subjection be whenas Dame For-
    tune please.
Of brittle joy, of smiling cheer, of honey mixed
    with gall,
Allotted is to every prince in freedom to be thrall:
What watches long, what sleeps unsure, what griefs
    and cares of mind,
What bitter broils, what endless toils, to kingdoms
    be assigned!

The subject then may well compare with prince
    for pleasant days,
Whose silent night brings quiet rest, whose steps
    no storm bewrays.
How much be we then bound to God, who such
    provision makes
To lay our cares upon the prince! Thus doth He
    for our sakes.
To Him therefore let us lift up our hearts and
    pray amain,
That every prince that He hath placed may long
    in quiet reign.

V.

OF A CONTENTED MIND.[1]

(By Thomas Lord Vaux.)

WHEN all is done and said,
    In the end thus shall you find,
He most of all doth bathe in bliss
    That hath a quiet mind,

And, clear from worldly cares,
    To deem can be content
The sweetest time in all his life
    In thinking to be spent.

The body subject is
    To fickle Fortune's power,
And to a million of mishaps
    Is casual every hour;

And death in time doth change
    It to a clod of clay,
Whenas the mind, which is divine,
    Runs never to decay.

Companion none is like
    Unto the mind alone;
For many have been harmed by speech;
    Through thinking few or none:

[1] "Paradise of Dainty Devices," 1576, &c.

Fear oftentimes restraineth words,
But makes not thoughts to cease,
And he speaks best that hath the skill
When for to hold his peace.

Our wealth leaves us at death;
Our kinsmen at the grave;
But virtues of the mind unto
The heavens with us we have.

Wherefore, for virtue's sake,
I can be well content
The sweetest time of all my life
To deem in thinking spent.

L. Vaux.

VI.

OF THE INSTABILITY OF YOUTH.[1]

(By Thomas Lord Vaux or J. Haryngton.)

WHEN I look back, and in myself behold
The wandering ways that youth could
not descry,
And mark the fearful course that youth
did hold,
And meet in mind each step youth strayed awry;
My knees I bow, and from my heart I call,—
O Lord, forget these faults and follies all!

[1] "Paradise of Dainty Devices," signed L. Vaux. Four
stanzas, much varied, claimed for J. Haryngton in " Nugæ
Antiquæ," vol. ii. p. 333, edit. Park.

For now I see how void youth is of skill;
　　I see also his prime time and his end;
I do confess my faults and all my ill,
　　And sorrow sore for that I did offend;
And with a mind repentant of all crimes,
Pardon I ask for youth ten thousand times.

The humble heart hath daunted the proud mind;
　　Eke wisdom hath given ignorance a fall;
And wit hath taught that folly could not find,
　　And age hath youth her subject and her thrall.
Therefore I pray, O Lord of life and truth,
Pardon the faults committed in my youth!

Thou that didst grant the wise king his request;
　　Thou that in whale thy prophet didst preserve;
Thou that forgavest the wounding of thy breast;
　　Thou that didst save the thief in state to starve;
Thou only God, the Giver of all Grace,
Wipe out of mind the path of youth's vain race!

Thou that by power to life didst raise the dead;
　　Thou that of grace restor'dst the blind to sight;
Thou that for love Thy life and love outbled;
　　Thou that of favour madest the lame go right;
Thou that canst heal and help in all assays,
Forgive the guilt that grew in youth's vain ways!

And now since I, with faith and doubtless mind,
　　Do fly to Thee by prayer to appease Thy ire,
And since that Thee I only seek to find,
　　And hope by faith to attain my just desire;
Lord, mind no more youth's error and unskill,
And able age to do Thy Holy Will!

VII.

ON ISABELLA MARKHAM.[1]

(By J. Haryngton. Before 1564?)

WHENCE comes my love? O heart, disclose!
'Twas from cheeks that shame the
    rose;
From lips that spoil the ruby's praise;
From eyes that mock the diamond's blaze.
Whence comes my woe? As freely own:
Ah me! 'twas from a heart of stone.

The blushing cheek speaks modest mind;
The lips, befitting words most kind;
The eye does tempt to love's desire,
And seems to say, 'tis Cupid's fire:
Yet all so fair but speak my moan,
Sith nought doth say the heart of stone.

Why thus, my love, so kind bespeak
Sweet lip, sweet eye, sweet blushing cheek,
Yet not a heart to save my pain?
O Venus! take thy gifts again!
Make not so fair to cause our moan;
Or make a heart that's like your own!

[1] "Nugæ Antiquæ," vol. ii. p. 324, edit. Park.

VIII.

VERSES MADE BY QUEEN ELIZABETH.[1]

(*Circ.* 1569.)

THE doubt of future foes
　　　Exiles my present joy,
And wit me warns to shun such snares
　　　As threaten mine annoy.

For falsehood now doth flow,
　　　And subject faith doth ebb,
Which would not be if reason ruled,
　　　Or wisdom weaved the web.

But clouds of toys untried
　　　Do cloak aspiring minds,
Which turn to rain of late repent,
　　　By course of changed winds.

The top of hope supposed
　　　The root of ruth will be,
And fruitless all their graffed guiles,
　　　As shortly ye shall see.

Then dazzled eyes with pride,
　　　Which great ambition blinds,
Shall be unscaled by worthy wights,
　　　Whose foresight falsehood finds.

[1] Printed by Puttenham, "Art of Poesy," 1589, p. 208, as a "ditty of her Majesty's own making, passing sweet and harmonical." In MS. Rawl. Poet. 108, fol. 44, *verso*, it is entitled "Verses made by the Queen's Majesty." Another text was printed by Brydges from a Harl. MS.; "Topographer," vol. ii. p. 176.

The daughter of debate,
That eke discord doth sow,
Shall reap no gain where former rule
Hath taught still peace to grow.

No foreign banished wight
Shall anchor in this port;
Our realm it brooks no stranger's force;
Let them elsewhere resort.

Our rusty sword with rest
Shall first his edge employ,
To poll their tops that seek such change,
And gape for future joy.

IX.

THREE SONNETS FROM THE WORKS OF

SIR PHILIP SIDNEY.

(Born 1554; died 1586.)

I.[1]

WITH how sad steps, O moon, thou
climb'st the skies!
How silently, and with how wan a
face!
What! may it be that even in heavenly place
That busy archer his sharp arrows tries?

[1] Gray's "Miscellaneous Works of Sidney," p. 87, from
"Astrophel and Stella." The first two lines adapted by
Wordsworth, "Miscellaneous Sonnets," No. 3.

Sure, if that long-with-love-acquainted eyes
   Can judge of love, thou feel'st a lover's case.
   I read it in thy looks; thy languished grace
To me, that feel the like, thy state descries.
Then, even of fellowship, O moon! tell me
   Is constant love deemed there but want of wit?
Are beauties there as proud as here they be?
   Do they above love to be loved, and yet
Those lovers scorn, whom that love doth possess?
Do they call virtue there ungratefulness?

II.[1]

COME, sleep; O sleep! the certain knot of peace,
   The baiting-place of wit, the balm of woe,
The poor man's wealth, the prisoner's release,
   The indifferent judge between the high and low;
With shield of proof, shield me from out the prease
   Of those fierce darts despair at me doth throw.
O make in me those civil wars to cease;
   I will good tribute pay if thou do so.
Take thou of me smooth pillows, sweetest bed,
   A chamber deaf to noise and blind to light,
A rosy garland and a weary head:
   And if these things, as being thine by right,
Move not thy heavy grace, thou shalt in me
Livelier than elsewhere Stella's image see.

III.[2]

LEAVE me, O love! which reachest but to dust,
   And thou, my mind, aspire to higher things!

---

[1] Gray's " Miscellaneous Works of Sidney," p. 92.
[2] Sidney's "Arcadia," p. 539, edit. 1674.

Grow rich in that which never taketh rust :
    Whatever fades, but fading pleasure brings.
Draw in thy beams, and humble all thy might
    To that sweet yoke where lasting freedoms be ;
Which breaks the clouds and opens forth the light ;
    That doth both shine, and give us sight to see.
O take fast hold ! Let that light be thy guide
    In this small course which birth draws out to
        death ;
And think how evil becometh him to slide
    Who seeketh Heaven, and comes of heavenly
        breath.
Then farewell, world ! thy uttermost I see:
Eternal Love, maintain thy life in me !

       Splendidis longum valedico nugis.

X.

PSALM LXIX.[1]

(From the translation of the Psalms by Sir Philip Sidney,
and his sister Mary, Countess of Pembroke.)

ROUBLOUS seas my soul surround :
    Save, O God ! my sinking soul,—
Sinking where it feels no ground,
    In this gulf, this whirling hole :
Waiting aid, with earnest eying,
Calling God with bootless crying ;

[1] From the edition of 1823, p. 120. This Psalm belongs
to the part which is generally ascribed to the Countess of
Pembroke.

Dim and dry in me are found
Eye to see and throat to sound.

Wrongly set to work my woe,
   Haters have I more than hairs :
Force in my afflicting foe
   Bettering still, in me impairs.
Thus to pay and leese constrained
What I never ought or gained,
Yet say I, Thou God dost know
How my faults and follies go.

Mighty Lord ! let not my case
   Blank the rest that hope in Thee !
Let not Jacob's God deface
   All His friends in blush of me !
Thine it is, Thine only quarrel
Dights me thus in shame's apparel :
Mote nor spot nor least disgrace,
But for Thee, could taint my face.

To my kin a stranger quite,
   Quite an alien am I grown ;
In my very brethren's sight
   Most uncared for, most unknown.
With Thy temple's zeal out-eaten,
With Thy slanders' scourges beaten,
While the shot of piercing spite,
Bent at Thee, on me doth light.

*   *   *   *   *   *

Unto Thee what needs be told
   My reproach, my blot, my blame ?
Sith both these Thou didst behold,
   And canst all my haters name.

Whiles afflicted, whiles heart-broken,
Waiting yet some friendship's token,
Some I looked would me uphold,—
Looked,—but found all comfort cold.

Comfort? nay, not seen before,
    Needing food they set me gall;
Vinegar they filled me store,
    When for drink my thirst did call.
O then snare them in their pleasures!
Make them trapt even in their treasures!
Gladly sad, and richly poor,
Sightless most, yet mightless more!

Down upon them fury rain!
    Lighten indignation down!
Turn to waste and desert plain
    House and palace, field and town!
Let not one be left abiding
Where such rancour had residing!
Whom Thou painest, more they pain;
Hurt by Thee, by them is slain.

*   *   *   *   *   *

XI.

FANCY AND DESIRE.[1]

(By Edward Earl of Oxford.   Born 1540? died 1604.)

OME hither, shepherd's swain !
      Sir, what do you require ?
    I pray thee, shew to me thy name !
      My name is Fond Desire.

When wert thou born, Desire ?
  In pomp and prime of May.
By whom, sweet boy, wert thou begot ?
  By fond Conceit, men say.

Tell me, who was thy nurse ?
  Fresh youth, in sugared joy.
What was thy meat and daily food ?
  Sad sighs, with great annoy.

What hadst thou then to drink ?
  Unfeigned lovers' tears.
What cradle wert thou rocked in ?
  In hope devoid of fears.

What lulled thee then asleep ?
  Sweet speech, which likes me best.
Tell me, where is thy dwelling-place ?
  In gentle hearts I rest.

[1] Given by Percy from Delouey's "Garland of Goodwill,"
p. 105, Percy Soc. ed.; by Ellis and others from Breton's
"Bower of Delights," 1597. A shorter copy in Puttenham's
"Art of Poesy," 1589, p. 172, as by "Edward, Earl of Ox-
ford, a most noble and learned gentleman." Also imper-
fectly in Harl. MS. 6910, fol. 145, and in MS. Rawl. 85,
fol. 15, *verso*.

What thing doth please thee most?
   To gaze on beauty still.
Whom dost thou think to be thy foe?
   Disdain of my good will.

   Doth company displease?
   Yes, surely, many one.
Where doth Desire delight to live?
   He loves to live alone.

   Doth either time or age
   Bring him unto decay?
No, no! Desire both lives and dies
   A thousand times a day.

   Then, fond Desire, farewell!
   Thou art no mate for me;
I should be loath, methinks, to dwell
   With such a one as thee.

XII.

IF WOMEN COULD BE FAIR, ETC.[1]

(By Edward Earl of Oxford.)

IF women could be fair, and yet not fond,
   Or that their love were firm, not
     fickle, still,
   I would not marvel that they make
men bond

---

[1] MS. Rawl. 85, fol. 16, as by the "Earl of Oxenford." Printed from that MS. by Dr. Bliss, Preface to Brydges' reprint of "England's Helicon," p. xxvi; and from him by many others, sometimes with the title "A Renunciation." A different copy was printed by Byrd in 1587; see "Cens. Lit." vol. ii. p. 114, second edit.

By service long to purchase their good will;
But when I see how frail those creatures are,
I muse that men forget themselves so far.

To mark the choice they make, and how they change,
　How oft from Phœbus they do flee to Pan,
Unsettled still, like haggards wild, they range,—
　These gentle birds that fly from man to man;
Who would not scorn and shake them from the fist,
And let them fly, fair fools, which way they list?

Yet, for disport, we fawn and flatter both,
　To pass the time when nothing else can please;
And train them to our lure with subtle oath,
　Till, weary of their wiles, ourselves we ease:
And then we say, when we their fancy try,
To play with fools, oh, what a fool was I!

.

.

XIII.

FAIN WOULD I SING, ETC.[1]

(By Edward Earl of Oxford.)

AIN would I sing, but Fury makes me fret,
　　And Rage hath sworn to seek revenge
　　　of wrong;
　My mazed mind in malice so is set,
As Death shall daunt my deadly dolours long:

[1] MS. Tann. 306, p. 193, as by the "Earl of Oxenford."
Printed from that MS. by Dr. Bliss, edit. of Wood's
"Fasti," vol. i. p. 177.

Patience perforce is such a pinching pain,
As die I will, or suffer wrong again.

I am no sot, to suffer such abuse
  As doth bereave my heart of his delight;
Nor will I frame myself to such as use
  With calm consent to suffer such despite:
No quiet sleep shall once possess mine eye,
Till Wit have wrought his will on injury.

My heart shall fail, and hand shall lose his force,
  But some device shall pay Despite his due;
And Fury shall consume my careful corse,
  Or raze the ground whereon my sorrow grew:
Lo! thus, in rage of ruthful mind refused,
I rest revenged of whom I am abused.

XIV.

THE EARL OF OXFORD TO THE READER OF

BEDINGFIELD'S CARDANUS.[1]

(1576.)

THE labouring man that tills the fertile
      soil,
  And reaps the harvest fruit, hath not
      indeed
The gain, but pain; and if for all his toil
  He gets the straw, the lord will have the seed.

[1] Prefixed to Bedingfield's translation of Cardanus's
"Comfort," 1576, which was "published by commandment
of the right honourable the Earl of Oxenford," who also has
a prefatory letter to the translator.

The manchet fine falls not unto his share;
 On coarsest cheat his hungry stomach feeds;
The landlord doth possess the finest fare;
 He pulls the flowers, the other plucks but weeds.

The mason poor that builds the lordly halls
 Dwells not in them; they are for high degree;
His cottage is compact in paper walls,
 And not with brick or stone as others be.

The idle drone that labours not at all
 Sucks up the sweet of honey from the bee;
Who worketh most, to their share least doth fall:
 With due desert reward will never be.

The swiftest hare unto the mastiff slow
 Oft-times doth fall to him as for a prey:
The greyhound thereby doth miss his game, we
  know,
 For which he made such speedy haste away.

So he that takes the pain to pen the book
 Reaps not the gifts of goodly golden Muse;
But those gain that who on the work shall look,
 And from the sour the sweet by skill doth choose:
For he that beats the bush the bird not gets,
But who sits still and holdeth fast the nets.

XV.

1.

EPIGRAM.[1]

(By Edward Earl of Oxford.)

WERE I a king, I could command content;
 Were I obscure, hidden should be
  my cares ;
 Or were I dead, no cares should me
torment,
 Nor hopes, nor hates, nor loves, nor griefs, nor
fears.
A doubtful choice,—of these three which to crave ;
A kingdom, or a cottage, or a grave.

2.

ANSWERED THUS BY Sr P. S.

WERT thou a king, yet not command
  content,
 Sith empire none thy mind could yet
  suffice ;
Wert thou obscure, still cares would thee torment;
 But wert thou dead, all care and sorrow dies.
An easy choice,—of these three which to crave ;
No kingdom, nor a cottage, but a grave.

[1] MS. Chetham 8012, p. 84. A copy of the first two epigrams, without distinction of authors, is printed from "an ancient MS. Miscellany" in Lord Orford's "Works," vol. i. p. 551, as Lord Oxford's, signed "Vere."

3.

ANOTHER, OF ANOTHER MIND.

A KING? oh, boon for my aspiring mind!
    A cottage makes a country swad
        rejoice;
    And as for death, I like him in his kind,
But God forbid that he should be my choice!
A kingdom or a cottage or a grave,—
Nor last, nor next, but first and best I crave;
The rest I can whenas I list enjoy,
Till then salute me thus,—*Vive le Roy!*

                        F. M.

4.

ANOTHER, OF ANOTHER MIND.

THE greatest kings do least command
    content;
    The greatest cares do still attend a
        crown;
A grave all happy fortunes do[th] prevent,
    Making the noble equal with the clown:
A quiet country life to lead I crave;
A cottage, then; no kingdom nor a grave.

XVI.

MY MIND TO ME A KINGDOM IS.[1]

(By Sir Edward Dyer. Born *circ.* 1540; died 1607.)

MY mind to me a kingdom is,
　　Such present joys therein I find,
　That it excels all other bliss
　　That earth affords or grows by kind :
Though much I want which most would have,
Yet still my mind forbids to crave.

No princely pomp, no wealthy store,
　　No force to win the victory,
No wily wit to salve a sore,　•
　　No shape to feed a loving eye ;
To none of these I yield as thrall :
For why?　My mind doth serve for all.

I see how plenty [surfeits] oft,
　　And hasty climbers soon do fall ;
I see that those which are aloft
　　Mishap doth threaten most of all ;
They get with toil, they keep with fear ;
Such cares my mind could never bear.

---

[1] From MS. Rawl. 85, p. 17. There is a very similar but anonymous copy in Brit. Mus. Addit. MS. 15,225, p. 85. Longer copies, also anonymous, are printed from Byrd in " Exc. Tudor." vol. i. pp. 100-1, and in " Cens. Lit." vol. ii. pp. 108-9 ; as well as by Percy, &c. There is an imitation in J. Sylvester's " Works," p. 651.

Content to live, this is my stay;
   I seek no more than may suffice;
I press to bear no haughty sway;
   Look, what I lack my mind supplies:
Lo, thus I triumph like a king,
Content with that my mind doth bring.

Some have too much, yet still do crave;
   I little have, and seek no more.
They are but poor, though much they have,
   And I am rich with little store:
They poor, I rich; they beg, I give;
They lack, I leave; they pine, I live.

I laugh not at another's loss;
   I grudge not at another's pain;
No worldly waves my mind can toss;
   My state at one doth still remain:
I fear no foe, I fawn no friend;
I loathe not life, nor dread my end.

Some weigh their pleasure by their lust,
   Their wisdom by their rage of will;
Their treasure is their only trust;
   A cloaked craft their store of skill:
But all the pleasure that I find
Is to maintain a quiet mind.

My wealth is health and perfect ease:
   My conscience clear my chief defence;
I neither seek by bribes to please,
   Nor by deceit to breed offence:
Thus do I live; thus will I die;
Would all did so as well as I!

               E. Dier.

XVII.

1.

THE SHEPHERD'S CONCEIT OF PROMETHEUS.[1]

(By Sir Edward Dyer.)

PROMETHEUS when first from heaven
        high
    He brought down fire, 'ere then on
        earth unseen,
Fond of the light, a satyr, standing by,
    Gave it a kiss, as it like sweet had been.

Feeling forthwith the other's burning power,
    Wood with the smart, with shouts and shriekings
        shrill,
He sought his ease in river, field and bower,
    But for the time his grief went with him still.

So silly I, with that unwonted sight
    In human shape, an angel from above,
Feeding mine eyes, the impression there did light,
    That since I run and rest as pleaseth love.

The difference is, the satyr's lips, my heart,—
He for a while, I evermore,—have smart.

[1] With Dyer's name in MS. Rawl. 85, p. 8, and "Eng-
land's Helicon," 1600; also headed E. D. in "the Countess
of Pembroke's Arcadia," p. 477, edit. 1598. An anonymous
copy in Harl. MS. 6910, fol. 154, *verso*.

2.

A REPLY.[1]

(By Sir Philip Sidney.)

 SATYR once did run away for dread,
     With sound of horn, which he him-
          self did blow;
Fearing and feared, thus from himself
     he fled,
Deeming strange evil in that he did not know.

Such causeless fears when coward minds do take,
     It makes them fly that which they fain would
          have;
As this poor beast, who did his rest forsake,
     Thinking not why, but how, himself to save.

Even thus mought I, for doubts which I conceive
     Of mine own words, mine own good hap betray;
And thus might I, for fear of maybe, leave
     The sweet pursuit of my desired prey.

Better like I thy satyr, dearest Dyer,
Who burnt his lips to kiss fair shining fire.

     [1] From the same copies as the preceding piece.

XVIII.

THE MAN WHOSE THOUGHTS, ETC.[1]

(By Sir Edward Dyer.)

THE man whose thoughts against him do
        conspire,
    In whom Mishap her story doth de-
        paint,
The man of woe, the matter of [desire],
    Free of the dead, that lives in endless plaint,
His spirit am I, which in this desert lie,
To rue his case, whose cause I cannot fly.

Despair my name, who never finds relief;
    Friended of none, but to myself a foe;
An idle care, maintained by firm belief
    That praise of faith shall through my torments
        grow;
And count those hopes, that others' hearts do ease,
But base conceits the common sense to please.

For sure I am I never shall attain
    The happy good from whence my joys arise;
Nor have I power my sorrows to restrain,
    But wail the want, when nought else may suffice;
Whereby my life the shape of death must bear,—
That death which feels the worst that life doth fear.

[1] MS. Rawl. 85, fol. 7, signed " M. Dier." Printed from
that MS. by Dr. Bliss, edit. of Wood's "A. O.," vol. i. p.
743.   There is an anonymous copy in Harl. MS. 6910, fol.
169.

But what avails with tragical cómplaint,
  Not hoping help, the Furies to awake?
Or why should I the happy minds acquaint
  With doleful tunes, their settled peace to shake?
All ye that here behold Infortune's fare,
May judge no woe may with my grief compare.

XIX.

A FANCY.[1]

(By Sir Edward Dyer.)

E that his mirth hath lost,
    Whose comfort is dismayed,
  Whose hope is vain, whose faith is
        scorned,
  Whose trust is all betrayed,

If he have held them dear,
And cannot cease to moan,
Come, let him take his place by me;
He shall not rue alone.

But if the smallest sweet
Be mixed with all his sour;

[1] MS. Rawl. Poet. 85, fol. 109, signed as below; MS. Tann. 306, fol. 173, with the same signature; MS. Ashm. 781, p. 140, signed " S^r Ed. Dyer;" and Harl. MS. 6910, fol. 159. Authenticated by Dyer himself through the secret signature near the end, and ascribed to him by R. Southwell in the poem which follows in this volume. Wrongly claimed for Lord Pembroke in the " Poems of Pembroke and Rud- yard," 1660, p. 29.

If in the day, the month, the year,
  He feel one lightening hour,

Then rest he by himself;
  He is no mate for me,
Whose hope is fallen, whose succour void,
  Whose hap his death must be.

Yet not the wished death,
  Which hath no plaint nor lack,
Which, making free the better part,
  Is only nature's wrack.

O no! that were too well;
  My death is of the mind,
Which always yields extremest pains,
  And leaves the worst behind.

As one that lives in show,
  But inwardly doth die,
Whose knowledge is a bloody field
  Where all hope slain doth lie;

Whose heart the altar is;
  Whose spirit, the sacrifice
Unto the powers, whom to appease
  No sorrow can suffice.

My fancies are like thorns,
  On which I go by night;
Mine arguments are like an host
  Which force hath put to flight.

My sense is passion's spy;
  My thoughts like ruins old
Of famous Carthage, or the town
  Which Sinon bought and sold;

Which still before mine eyes
    My mortal fall do lay,
Whom love and fortune once advanced,
    And now hath cast away.

O thoughts, no thoughts, but wounds,
    Sometime the seat of joy,
Sometime the seat of quiet rest,
    But now of all annoy.

I sowed the soil of peace;
    My bliss was in the spring;
And day by day I ate the fruit
    Which my life's tree did bring.

To nettles now my corn,
    My field is turned to flint,
Where, sitting in the cypress shade,
    I read the hyacint.

The peace, the rest, the life,
    That I enjoyed before
Came to my lot, that by the loss
    My smart might sting the more.

So to unhappy men
    The best frames to the worst;
O time, O place, O words, O looks,
    Dear then, but now accurst!

In *was* stands my delight;
    In *is* and *shall*, my woe;
My horror fastens on the *yea*;
    My hope hangs on the *no*.

I look for no relief;
Relief would come too late;
Too late I find, I find too well,
Too well stood my estate.

Behold, such is the end;
What thing may here be sure?
O, nothing else but plaints and moans
Do to the end endure.

Forsaken first was I,
Then utterly forgotten;
And he that came not to my faith,
Lo! my reward hath gotten.

Then, Love, where is the sauce
That makes thy torment sweet?
Where is the cause that some have thought
Their death through thee but meet?

The stately chaste disdain,
The secret shamefastness,
The grace reserved, the common light
Which shines in worthiness.

O would it were not so,
Or I it might excuse!
O would the wrath of jealousy
My judgment might abuse!

O frail inconstant kind,
O safe in trust to no man!
No women angels be, and lo!
My mistress is a woman!

Yet hate I but the fault,
And not the faulty one,
Nor can I rid me of the bands
Wherein I lie alone.

Alone I lie, whose like
Was never seen as yet;
The prince, the poor, the old, the young,
The fond, the full of wit.

Hers still remain must I,
By wrong, by death, by shame;
I cannot blot out of my mind
That love wrought in her name.

I cannot set at nought
That once I held so dear;
I cannot make it seem so far
That is indeed so near.

Not that I mean henceforth
This strange will to profess,
As one that would betray such troth,
And build on fickleness.

But it shall never fail
That my faith bare in hand;
I gave my word, my word gave me;
Both word and gift must stand!

Sith then it must be thus,
And thus is all-to ill,
I yield me captive to my curse,
My hard fate to fulfil.

The solitary woods
My city shall become ;
The darkest den shall be my lodge,
  Wherein I'll rest or roam.

Of heben black my board ;
The worms my feast shall be,
On which my carcass shall be fed
  Till they do feed on me ;

My wine of Niobe,
My bed of craggy rock,
'The serpent's hiss my harmony,
  The shrieking owl my clock.

My exercise nought else
But raging agonies ;
My books of spiteful Fortune's foils
  And dreary tragedies.

My walk the paths of plaint,
My prospect into hell,
Where wretched Sisyphe and his pheres
  In endless pains do dwell.

And though I seem to use
The poet's feigned style,
To figure forth my rueful plight,
  My fall or my exile,

Yet is my grief not feigned,
In which I starve and pine ;
Who feel it most shall find it least
  If his compare with mine.

My Muse if any ask,
Whose grievous case was such?
Dy ERE thou let his name be known;
His folly shows so much.

But best 'twere thee to hide,
And never come to light;
For on the earth may none but I
This action sound aright.

Miserum est fuisse.

E. DIER.

XX.

MASTER DYER'S FANCY TURNED TO A SINNER'S COMPLAINT.[1]

(By Robert Southwell. Born 1560; died 1595.)

E that his mirth hath lost,
    Whose comfort is to rue,
  Whose hope is fallen, whose faith is
        crazed,
Whose trust is found untrue;

If he have held them dear,
  And cannot cease to moan,
Come, let him take his place by me;
  He shall not rue alone.

[1] Southwell's "Poems," edit. 1630, sign. F 7, &c., with the title, "A Fancy turned to a Sinner's Complaint." The title which I have adopted is found in the MS. of Southwell's poems used in both the modern editions, of Walter, p. 84, and Turnbull, p. 81.

But if the smallest sweet
Be mixed with all his sour;
If in the day, the month, the year,
He feels one lightening hour,

Then rest he with himself;
He is no mate for me,
Whose time in tears, whose race in ruth,
Whose life a death must be.

Yet not the wished death,
That feels no pain or lack,
That, making free the better part,
Is only nature's wrack:

O no! that were too well;
My death is of the mind,
That always yields extremest pangs,
Yet threatens worse behind.

As one that lives in show,
And inwardly doth die;
Whose knowledge is a bloody field,
Where Virtue slain doth lie;

Whose heart the altar is,
And host, a God to move;
From whom my ill doth fear revenge,
His good doth promise love.

My fancies are like thorns.
In which I go by night;
My frighted wits are like an host
That force hath put to flight.

M

My sense is passion's spy;
My thoughts like ruins old,
Which show how fair the building was,
While grace did it uphold.

And still before mine eyes
My mortal fall they lay:
Whom grace and virtue once advanced,
Now sin hath cast away.

O thoughts, no thoughts, but wounds,
Sometime the seat of joy,
Sometime the store of quiet rest,
But now of all annoy.

I sowed the soil of peace;
My bliss was in the spring;
And day by day the fruit I ate,
That virtue's tree did bring.

To nettles now my corn,
My field is turned to flint,
Where I a heavy harvest reap
Of cares that never stint.

The peace, the rest, the life,
That I enjoyed of yore,
Were happy lot, but by their loss
My smart doth sting the more.

So to unhappy men
The best frames to the worst:
O time, O place, where thus I fell,
Dear then, but now accurst!

In *was* stands my delight;
In *is* and *shall*, my woe;
My horror fastened in the *yea*;
My hope hangs in the *no*.

Unworthy of relief,
That craved is too late,
Too late I find, I find too well,
Too well stood my estate.

Behold, such is the end
That Pleasure doth procure;
Of nothing else but care and plaint
Can she the mind assure.

Forsaken first by Grace,
By Pleasure now forgotten,
Her pain I feel, but Grace's wage
Have others from me gotten.

Then, Grace, where is the joy
That makes thy torments sweet?
Where is the cause that many thought
Their deaths through thee but meet?

Where thy disdain of sin,
Thy secret sweet delight,
Thy sparks of bliss, thy heavenly joys,
That shined erst so bright?

O that they were not lost,
Or I could it excuse!
O that a dream of feigned loss
My judgment did abuse!

O frail inconstant flesh,´
    Soon trapped in every gin !
Soon wrought thus to betray thy soul,
    And plunge thyself in sin !

    Yet hate I but the fault,
    And not the faulty one,
Nor can I rid from me the mate
    That forceth me to moan ;

    To moan a sinner's case,
    Than which was never worse,
In prince or poor, in young or old,
    In blest or full of curse.

    Yet God's must I remain,
    By death, by wrong, by shame ;
I cannot blot out of my heart
    That Grace writ in His name.

    I cannot set at nought
    Whom I have held so dear ;
I cannot make Him seem afar,
    That is indeed so near.

Not that I look henceforth
    For love that erst I found ;
Sith that I brake my plighted troth
    To build on fickle ground.

    Yet that shall never fail
    Which my faith bare in hand;
I gave my vow ; my vow gave me ;
    Both vow and gift shall stand.

But since that I have sinned,
And scourge none is too ill,
I yield me captive to my curse,
    My hard fate to fulfil.

The solitary wood
My city shall become;
The darkest dens shall be my lodge;
    In which I rest or come;

A sandy plot my board,
The worms my feast shall be,
Wherewith my carcass shall be fed,
    Until they feed on me.

My tears shall be my wine,
My bed a craggy rock.
My harmony the serpent's hiss,
    The screeching owl my clock.

My exercise, remorse,
And doleful sinners' lays;
My book, remembrance of my crimes,
    And faults of former days.

My walk, the path of plaint;
My prospect into hell,
Where Judas and his cursed crew
    In endless pains do dwell.

And though I seem to use
The feigning poet's style,
To figure forth my careful plight,
    My fall and my exile;

Yet is my grief not feigned,
    Wherein I starve and pine;
Who feels the most shall think it least,
    If his compare with mine.

XXI.

WHO GRACE FOR ZENITH HAD.[1]

ANOTHER ADAPTATION OF SIR E. DYER'S FANCY.

(By Fulke Greville, Lord Brooke. Born 1554;
died 1628.)

WHO grace for zenith had,
    From which no shadows grow,
Who hath seen joy of all his hopes,
    And end of all his woe;

Whose love beloved hath been
    The crown of his desire;
Who hath seen sorrow's glories burnt
    In sweet affection's fire;

If from this heavenly state,
    Which souls with souls unites,
He be fallen down into the dark
    Despaired war of sprites,

Let him lament with me;
    For none doth glory know,
That hath not been above himself,
    And thence fallen down to woe.

[1] "Cœlica," Sonnet LXXXIII, in Lord Brooke's "Works."
1633, pp. 228-233.

But if there be one hope
Left in his languished heart,
If fear of worse, if wish of ease,
If horror may depart,

He plays with his complaints;
He is no mate for me,
Whose love is lost, whose hopes are fled,
Whose fears for ever be:

Yet not those happy fears
Which show Desire her death,
Teaching with use a peace in woe,
And in despair a faith.

No, no; my fears kill not,
But make uncured wounds,
Where joy and peace do issue out,
And only pain abounds.

Unpossible are help,
Reward, and hope to me;
Yet while unpossible they are,
They easy seem to be.

Most easy seems remorse,
Despair, and death to me;
Yet while they passing easy seem,
Unpossible they be.

So neither can I leave
My hopes that do deceive,
Nor can I trust mine own despair
And nothing else receive.

Thus be unhappy men
Blest, to be more accurst;
Near to the glories of the sun
Clouds with most horror burst.

Like ghosts raised out of graves,
Who live not, though they go,
Whose walking fear to others is,
And to themselves a woe;

So is my life by her
Whose love to me is dead,
On whose worth my despair yet walks,
And my desire is fed.

I swallow down the bait
Which carries down my death;
I cannot put love from my heart
While life draws in my breath.

My winter is within,
Which withereth my joy;
My knowledge, seat of civil war,
Where friends and foes destroy;

And my desires are wheels,
Whereon my heart is borne,
With endless turning of themselves,
Still living to be torn.

My thoughts are eagle's food,
Ordained to be a prey
To [wrath], and being still consumed,
Yet never to decay.

My memory, where once
My heart laid up the store
Of help, of joy, of spirit's wealth,
To multiply them more,

Is now become the tomb
Wherein all these lie slain;
My help, my joy, my spirit's wealth
All sacrificed to pain.

In Paradise I once
Did live, and taste the tree,
Which shadowed was from all the world,
In joy to shadow me:

The tree hath lost his fruit,
Or I have lost my seat;
My soul both black with shadow is,
And over-burnt with heat.

Truth here for triumph serves,
To show her power is great,
Whom no desert can overcome,
Nor no distress entreat.

Time past lays up my joy,
And time to come my grief;
She ever must be my desire,
And never my relief.

Wrong, her lieutenant is;
My wounded thoughts are they
Who have no power to keep the field,
Nor will to run away.

O rueful constancy !
And where is change so base,
As it may be compared with thee
    In scorn and in disgrace?

    Like as the kings forlorn,
    Deposed from their estate,
Yet cannot choose but love the crown,
    Although new kings they hate ;

    If they do plead their right,—
    Nay, if they only live,—
Offences to the crown alike
    Their good and ill shall give.

    So I would I were not,
    Because I may complain,
And cannot choose but love my wrongs,
    And joy to wish in vain.

    This faith condemneth me ;
    My right doth rumour move ;
I may not know the cause I fell,
    Nor yet without cause love.

    Then, love, where is reward,—
    At least where is the fame
Of them that, being, bear thy cross,
    And, being not, thy name ?

    The world's example I,
    A fable everywhere,
A well from whence the springs are dried,
    A tree that doth not bear ;

I, like the bird in cage,
At first with cunning caught,
And in my bondage for delight
With greater cunning taught.

Now owner's humour dies ;
I neither loved, nor fed,
Nor freed am, till in the cage
Forgotten I be dead.

The ship of Greece, the stream,
And she be not the same
They were, although ship, stream, and she
Still bear their antique name.

The wood which was, is worn ;
Those waves are run away ;
Yet still a ship, and still a stream,
Still running to a sea.

She loved, and still she loves,
But doth not still love me ;
To all except myself yet is
As she was wont to be.

O my once happy thoughts !
The heaven where grace did dwell !
My saint hath turned away her face ;
And made that heaven my hell !

A hell, for so is that
From whence no souls return,
Where, while our spirits are sacrificed,
They waste not, though they burn.

Since then this is my state,
　　And nothing worse than this,
Behold the map of death-like life,
　　Exiled from lovely bliss:

　　Alone among the world,
　　Strange with my friends to be,
Showing my fall to them that scorn,
　　See not, or will not see;

　　My heart a wilderness,
　　My studies only fear,
And, as in shadows of curst death,
　　A prospect of despair.

　　My exercise must be
　　My horrors to repeat;
My peace, joy, end, and sacrifice,
　　Her dead love to entreat;

　　My food, the time that was;
　　The time to come, my fast;
For drink, the barren thirst I feel
　　Of glories that are past;

　　Sighs and salt tears my bath;
　　Reason my looking-glass,
To show me he most wretched is
　　That once most happy was.

　　Forlorn desires my clock,
　　To tell me every day
That Time hath stolen love, life, and all
　　But my distress away.

For music, heavy sighs;
My walk an inward woe;
Which like a shadow ever shall
Before my body go.

And I myself am he
That doth with none compare,
Except in woes and lack of worth
Whose states more wretched are.

Let no man ask my name,
Nor what else I should be;
For GRIEVE-ILL, pain, forlorn estate.
Do best decipher me.

XXII.

MONTANUS' FANCY

GRAVEN UPON THE BARK OF A TALL BEECH TREE.[1]

(By Thomas Lodge.   Born 1555? died 1625.)

FIRST shall the heavens want starry light;
 The seas be robbed of their waves;
 The day want sun, and sun want bright;
 The night want shade, the dead men
   graves;
The April flowers and leaf and tree,
Before I false my faith to thee.

[1] From Lodge's "Rosalind; Euphues' Golden Legacy,"
1590, 1592, &c.   Reprinted in Collier's "Shakespeare's
Library," 1843.

First shall the tops of highest hills
  By humble plains be overpried,
And poets scorn the Muses' quills,
  And fish forsake the water glide,
And Iris lose her coloured weed,
Before I fail thee at thy need.

First direful Hate shall turn to Peace,
  And Love relent in deep disdain,
And Death his fatal stroke shall cease,
  And Envy pity every pain,
And Pleasure mourn, and Sorrow smile,
Before I talk of any guile.

First Time shall stay his stayless race,
  And Winter bless his brows with corn,
And snow bemoisten July's face,
  And Winter spring, and Summer mourn,
Before my pen, by help of Fame,
Cease to recite thy sacred name.

XXIII.

THE SHEPHERD TO THE FLOWERS.[1]

(Before 1593.)

SWEET violets, Love's Paradise, that spread
      Your gracious odours, which you couched bear
  Within your paly faces,

---

[1] "Phœnix Nest," 1593, p. 95; "England's Helicon,"
1600, sign. T, signed "Ignoto." Thence in Brydges' and
the Oxford editions of Raleigh's "Poems."

Upon the gentle wing of some calm-breathing wind
  That plays amidst the plain ;
If, by the favour of propitious stars, you gain
Such grace as in my lady's bosom place to find,
  Be proud to touch those places !
And when her warmth your moisture forth doth wear,
Whereby her dainty parts are sweetly fed,
You, honours of the flowery meads, I pray,—
  You, pretty daughters of the earth and sun,—
With mild and seemly breathing straight display
  My bitter sighs, that have my heart undone!

Vermilion roses, that, with new day's rise
Display your crimson folds fresh-looking fair,
  Whose radiant bright disgraces
The rich adorned rays of roseate rising morn ;
  Ah, if her virgin's hand
  Do pluck your pure ere Phœbus view the land,
And veil your gracious pomp in lovely Nature's
      scorn ;
  If chance my mistress traces
Fast by your flowers to take the summer's air ;
Then, woeful blushing, tempt her glorious eyes
To spread their tears, Adonis' death reporting;
  And tell love's torments, sorrowing for her friend,
Whose drops of blood, within your leaves consorting,
  Report fair Venus' moans to have no end !
Then may remorse, in pitying of my smart,
Dry up my tears, and dwell within her heart.

XXIV.

THERE IS NONE, O, NONE BUT YOU!![1]

(By Robert Earl of Essex. Born 1567; died 1601.)

THERE is none, O, none but you,
  Who from me estrange the sight,
Whom mine eyes affect to view,
  And chained ears hear with delight.

Others' beauties others move:
  In you I all the graces find;
Such are the effects of love,
  To make them happy that are kind.

Women in frail beauty trust;
  Only seem you kind to me!
Still be truly kind and just,
  For that can't dissembled be.

Dear, afford me then your sight!
  That, surveying all your looks,
Endless volumes I may write,
  And fill the world with envied books,

Which when after ages view,
  All shall wonder and despair,—
Women, to find a man so true,
  And men, a woman half so fair!

[1] Printed from Aubrey's MSS. by Dr. Bliss, edit. of Wood's "Fasti," vol. i. p. 245.

XXV.

A PASSION OF MY LORD OF ESSEX.[1]

APPY were he could finish forth his fate
    In some unhaunted desert, most
      obscure
    From all societies, from love and hate
Of worldly folk; then might he sleep secure;
Then wake again, and ever give God praise,
    Content with hips and haws and bramble-berry;
In contemplation spending all his days,
    And change of holy thoughts to make him merry;
Where, when he dies, his tomb may be a bush,
Where harmless robin dwells with gentle thrush.

XXVI.

VERSES MADE BY THE EARL OF
ESSEX IN HIS TROUBLE.[2]

HE ways on earth have paths and turn-
    ings known;
    The ways on sea are gone by needle's
      light;

[1] MS. Ashm. 781, p. 83, as "Certain Verses made by Lord Essex;" and Chetham MS. 8012, p. 86, with the title given above. It is said to have been enclosed in a letter to the Queen from Ireland, in 1599, and has been frequently printed.

[2] Printed from a Brit. Mus. MS. by Ellis, "Specimens," vol. ii. p. 361, edit. 1811; and Devereux, "Earls of Essex," vol. ii. p. 111.

The birds of the air the nearest way have flown,
  And under earth the moles do cast aright ;
A way more hard than these I needs must take,
  Where none can teach, nor no man can direct ;
Where no man's good for me example makes,
  But all men's faults do teach *her* to suspect.
Her thoughts and mine such disproportion have ;
  All strength of love is infinite in me ;
She useth the advantage time and fortune gave
  Of worth and power to get the liberty.
Earth, sea, heaven, hell, are subject unto laws,
But I, poor I, must suffer and know no cause.

R. E. E.

XXVII.

TO TIME.[1]

(By A. W.   Before 1602.)

ETERNAL Time! that wastest without
        waste,
      That art, and art not,—diest, and
        livest still ;
Most slow of all, and yet of greatest haste ;
  Both ill and good, and neither good nor ill :
How can I justly praise thee or dispraise ?
Dark are thy nights, but bright and clear thy days.

---

[1] Davison's " Poetical Rhapsody," 1602, &c., p. 137, edit.
1621.

Both free and scarce, thou givest and takest again;
  Thy womb, that all doth breed, is tomb to all;
What so by thee hath life by thee is slain;
  From thee do all things rise, to thee they fall:
Constant, inconstant; moving, standing still;
Was, is, shall be, do thee both breed and kill.

I lose thee, while I seek to find thee out;
  The farther off, the more I follow thee;
The faster hold, the greater cause of doubt;
  Was, is, I know; but *shall,* I cannot see:
All things by thee are measured, thou by none;
All are in thee; thou in thyself alone.

XXVIII.

UPON AN HEROICAL POEM.

WHICH HE HAD BEGUN (IN IMITATION OF VIRGIL)

OF THE FIRST INHABITING THIS FAMOUS

ISLE BY BRUTE AND THE TROJANS.[1]

(By A. W. Before 1602.)

Y wanton Muse, that whilome wont to sing
    Fair Beauty's praise and Venus' sweet
      delight,
  Of late had changed the tenour of her
    string
  To higher tunes than serve for Cupid's fight:

[1] Davison's "Poetical Rhapsody," 1602, &c., p. 25, edit.
1621. Also in the second edition of "England's Helicon,"
1612, as "An Heroical Poem," with the signature "Ignoto."
Thence in Brydges' and the Oxford editions of Raleigh's
"Poems."

Shrill trumpets' sound, sharp swords, and lances
      strong,
War, blood, and death were matter of her song.

The god of love by chance had heard thereof,
    That I was proved a rebel to his crown:
Fit words for war! quoth he, with angry scoff;
    A likely man to write of Mars his frown!
Well are they sped whose praises he will write,
Whose wanton pen can nought but love indite!

This said, he whisked his party-coloured wings,
    And down to earth he comes, more swift than
        thought;
Then to my heart in angry haste he flings,
    To see what change these news of wars had
        wrought:
He pries and looks,—he ransacks every vein,—
Yet finds he nought save love and lover's pain.

Then I, that now perceived his needless fear,
    With heavy smile began to plead my cause:—
In vain, quoth I, this endless grief I bear,
    In vain I strive to keep thy grievous laws,
If, after proof so often trusty found,
Unjust suspect condemn me as unsound.

Is this the guerdon of my faithful heart?
    Is this the hope on which my life is stayed?
Is this the ease of never-ceasing smart?
    Is this the price that for my pains is paid?
Yet better serve fierce Mars in bloody field,
Where death or conquest end or joy doth yield.

Long have I served; what is my pay but pain?
    Oft have I sued; what gain I but delay?

My faithful love is 'quited with disdain;
   My grief a game, my pen is made a play;
Yea, Love, that doth in other favour find,
In me is counted madness out of kind.

And last of all—but grievous most of all,—
   Thyself, sweet Love, hath killed me with suspect:
Could Love believe that I from Love would fall?
   Is war of force to make me Love neglect?
No! Cupid knows my mind is faster set,
Than that by war I should my Love forget.

My Muse, indeed, to war inclines her mind:
   The famous acts of worthy Brute to write,
To whom the Gods this island's rule assigned,
   Which long he sought by seas through Neptune's
       spite:
With such conceits my busy head doth swell,
But in my heart nought else but Love doth dwell.

And in this war, thy part is not the least:
   Here shall my Muse Brute's noble love declare:
Here shalt thou see thy double love increased,
   Of fairest twins that ever lady bare;
Let Mars triumph in armour shining bright,
His conquered arms shall be thy triumph's light.

As he the world, so thou shalt him subdue,
   And I thy glory through the world will ring;
So by my pains thou wilt vouchsafe to rue,
   And kill despair.—With that he whisked his wing
And bade me write, and promised wished rest;
But sore I fear false hope will be the best.

XXIX.

SONNET

PREFIXED TO HIS MAJESTY'S INSTRUCTIONS TO HIS

DEAREST SON, HENRY THE PRINCE.[1]

(By King James I.)

GOD gives not kings the style of gods in
vain,
 For on His Throne His sceptre do
they sway;
 And as their subjects ought them to obey,
So kings should fear and serve their God again.
If then ye would enjoy a happy reign,
 Observe the statutes of your Heavenly King,
 And from His Law make all your laws to spring,
Since His lieutenant here ye should remain:
Reward the just; be steadfast, true, and plain;
 Repress the proud, maintaining aye the right;
 Walk always so as ever in His sight,
Who guards the godly, plaguing the profane.
 And so ye shall in princely virtues shine,
 Resembling right your mighty King divine.

[1] "Works of King James," by Bishop Montague, 1616,
p. 137.

XXX.

VERSES ADDRESSED TO KING JAMES I.[1]

(By Sir Arthur Gorges. Jan. 1, 1609-(10).)

F many now that sound with hope's
    consort
    Your wisdom, bounty, and peace-
        blessed reign,
My skill is least; but of the most import,
    Because not schooled by favours, gifts, or gain :
And, that which more approves my truthful lays,
    To sweet my tunes I strain not flattery's string,
But hold that temper in your royal praise
    That long I did, before you were my king;
As one that virtue for itself regards,
And loves his king more than his king's rewards.

XXXI.

EPITAPHS ON PRINCE HENRY.[2]

(Died Nov. 6, 1612.)

I.

AIR Britain's Prince, in the April of his
    years,
    The heaven, enamoured with his
        springing grace,

[1] Printed from the original MS. in the British Museum, in "Restituta," vol. iv. p. 509.

[2] "Mausoleum, or the choicest flowers of the Epitaphs" on Prince Henry; Edinburgh, 1613; reprinted by Mr. D. Laing, 1825.

Reft to herself for to enrich the spheres,
  And shine next Cynthia in the starry chase.
  And well enjoy he might so high a place;
For frowning Neptune's liquid field of fears,
And this poor mote of dust that all upbears,
  To his great mind seemed too-too small a space.
Yet it his corse doth keep; dear pledge! o'er which
  Affection's flames huge pyramids doth raise,
  All graven with golden letters of his praise.
But, ah! deprived of a gem so rich,
  Great Britain now but great to all appears
  In her great loss, and oceans of tears.

IGNOTO.

II.

WHY, pilgrim, dost thou stray
          By Asia's floods renowned;
          Or where great Atlas, crowned
      With clouds, him reaches 'bove heaven's
          milky way,
  Strange wonders to behold?
By Isis' streams if thou'lt but deign to stay,
  One thou shalt find surpassing all the told;
For there's in little room
The prince of men['s], and man of princes', tomb.

IGNOTO.

III.

ERE lies the world's delight,
    Dead to our sight, but in eternal light.
      These nine who by him moan,
        The Muses were, alas!
But, through his fatal case,
Are changed like wailing Niobe in stone.
      She, clad in sable robes,
      Who, in a deadly sleep,
Such pearly streams pours from her crystal globes,
      Is Virtue, that complains
She wanteth Argus' hundred eyes to weep,
      Or Iris' silver rains.
That winged Penthesileia in the air
    . Fame is, his praise who rolls
      'Twixt both the starry poles.
With earnest eyes to skies, and bay-crowned hair,
      Installed on Virtue's throne,
This ghostly sire that tramples pale Despair,
Brave Honour's called, who scorns to give a groan;
For in the programme of his life he reads,
Men's hopes of Him surmount Alcides' deeds.

IGNOTO.   .

XXXII.

THE MIND OF THE FRONTISPIECE TO RALEIGH'S HISTORY OF THE WORLD.[1]

(By Ben Jonson. 1614.)

FROM death and dark oblivion, near the
            same,
    The mistress of man's life, grave
            History,
Raising the world to good or evil fame,
    Doth vindicate it to Eternity.

High Providence would so, that nor the good
    Might be defrauded, nor the great secured;
But both might know their ways are understood,
    And the reward and punishment assured.

This makes that, lighted by the beamy hand
    Of Truth, which searcheth the most hidden springs,
And guided by Experience, whose straight wand
    Doth mete, whose line doth sound, the depth of
            things,

She cheerfully supporteth what she rears,
·   Assisted by no strengths but are her own;
Some note of which each varied pillar bears,
    By which, as proper titles, she is known—

Time's Witness, Herald of Antiquity,
The Light of Truth, and Life of Memory.

---

[1] Prefixed anonymously to Raleigh's "History," but claimed in Ben Jonson's "Underwoods," No. xlii., with several variations.

XXXIII.

TO THE KING[1]

(CHARLES I.).

(By George Sandys. Born 1577; died 1644.)

UR graver Muse from her long dream
    awakes;
Peneian groves and Cirrha's caves
    forsakes;
Inspired with zeal, she climbs the ethereal hills
Of Solyma, where bleeding balm distils;
Where trees of life unfading youth assure,
And living waters all diseases cure;
Where the sweet singer, in celestial lays,
Sung to his solemn harp Jehovah's praise.
From that fallen Temple on her wings she bears
Those heavenly raptures to your sacred ears.
Not that her bare and humble feet aspire
To mount the threshold of the harmonious choir;
But that at once she might oblations bring
To God, and tribute to a god-like king.
And since no narrow verse such mysteries,
Deep sense, and high expressions could comprise,
Her labouring wings a larger compass fly,
And Poesy resolves with Poesy;
Lest she, who in the Orient clearly rose,
Should in your Western world obscurely close.

[1] Prefixed to Sandys' "Paraphrase upon the Psalms of
David," 1636.

XXXIV.

DEO OPT. MAX.[1]

(By George Sandys.)

THOU, who all things hast of nothing
          made,
Whose hand the radiant firmament dis-
          played,
With such an undiscerned swiftness hurled
About the steadfast centre of the world;
Against whose rapid course the restless sun,
And wandering flames in varied motions run,
Which heat, light, life infuse; time, night, and day
Distinguish; in our human bodies sway:
That hung'st the solid earth in fleeting air,
Veined with clear springs. which ambient seas repair.
In clouds the mountains wrap their hoary heads;
Luxurious valleys clothed with flowery meads;
Her trees yield fruit and shade; with liberal breasts
All creatures she, their common mother, feasts.
Then man Thy image madest; in dignity,
In knowledge, and in beauty, like to Thee;
Placed in a heaven on earth; without his toil
The ever-flourishing and fruitful soil
Unpurchased food produced; all creatures were
His subjects, serving more for love than fear.
He knew no lord but Thee; but when he fell
From his obedience, all at once rebel,

---

[1] Appended to the same, pp. 240-4.

And in his ruin exercise their might;
Concurring elements against him fight;
Troops of unknown diseases, sorrow, age,
And death assail him with successive rage.
Hell let forth all her furies; none so great
As man to man:—ambition, pride, deceit,
Wrong armed with power, lust, rapine, slaughter
  reigned,
And flattered vice the name of virtue gained.
Then hills beneath the swelling waters stood,
And all the globe of earth was but one flood,
Yet could not cleanse their guilt. The following race
Worse than their fathers, and their sons more base;
Their god-like beauty lost; sin's wretched thrall;
No spark of their divine original
Left unextinguished; all enveloped
With darkness; in their bold transgressions dead:
When Thou didst from the East a light display,
Which rendered to the world a clearer day;
Whose precepts from Hell's jaws our steps withdraw,
And whose example was a living law;
Who purged us with His blood; the way prepared
To Heaven, and those long chained-up doors
  unbarred.
How infinite Thy mercy! which exceeds
The world thou madest, as well as our misdeeds;
Which greater reverence than Thy justice wins,
And still augments Thy honour by our sins.
O who hath tasted of Thy clemency
In greater measure or more oft than I!
My grateful verse Thy goodness shall display,
O Thou who went'st along in all my way,
To where the morning with perfumed wings

From the high mountains of Panchæa springs;
To that new found-out world, where sober Night
Takes from the Antipodes her silent flight;
To those dark seas where horrid Winter reigns.
And binds the stubborn floods in icy chains;
To Libyan wastes, whose thirst no showers assuage,
And where swoln Nilus cools the lion's rage.
Thy wonders in the deep have I beheld;
Yet all by those on Judah's hills excelled,
There, where the Virgin's Son His doctrine taught,
His miracles and our redemption wrought;
Where I, by Thee inspired, His praises sung,
And on His Sepulchre my offering hung.
Which way soe'er I turn my face or feet,
I see Thy glory, and Thy mercy meet;
Met on the Thracian shores, when in the strife
Of frantic Simoans Thou preservedst my life;
So, when Arabian thieves belaid us round,
And when, by all abandoned, Thee I found.
That false Sidonian wolf, whose craft put on
A sheep's soft fleece, and me, Bellerophon,
To ruin by his cruel letter sent,
Thou didst by Thy protecting hand prevent.
Thou savedst me from the bloody massacres
Of faithless Indians; from their treacherous wars;
From raging fevers; from the sultry breath
Of tainted air, which cloyed the jaws of death;
Preserved from swallowing seas, when towering
          waves
Mixed with the clouds, and opened their deep
          graves;
From barbarous pirates ransomed; by those taught,
Successfully with Salian Moors we fought;

Then brought'st me home in safety, that this earth
Might bury me, which fed me from my birth;
Blest with a healthful age, a quiet mind;
Content with little; to this work designed;
Which I at length have finished by Thy aid,
And now my vows have at Thy altar paid.

XXXV.

A HYMN TO MY REDEEMER.[1]

(By George Sandys.)

SAVIOUR of mankind, Man, Emmanuel,
Who sinless died for sin, who van-
quished hell,
The first-fruits of the grave; whose
life did give
Light to our darkness; in whose death we live; ·
O strengthen Thou my faith! Correct my will,
That mine may Thine obey! Protect me still,
So that the latter death may not devour
My soul, sealed with Thy seal! So in the hour
When Thou, whose body sanctified this tomb,
Unjustly judged, a glorious Judge shalt come
To judge the world with justice, by that sign
I may be known, and entertained for Thine!

[1] Sandys' "Relation of a Journey begun A. D. 1610," 1615, p. 167. These are the lines referred to in the last poem, as an offering hung upon the sepulchre of Christ.

XXXVI.

LORD STRAFFORD'S MEDITATIONS IN THE TOWER.[1]

(Author unknown.   1641.)

I.

GO, empty joys,
With all your noise,
And leave me here alone,
In sad sweet silence to bemoan
The fickle worldly height,
Whose danger none can see aright,
Whilst your false splendours dim the sight.

II.

Go, and ensnare
With your trim ware
Some other worldly wight,
And cheat him with your flattering light;
Rain on his head a shower
Of honour, greatness, wealth, and power;
Then snatch it from him in an hour.

---

[1] "Topographer," vol. ii. p. 234, from a Harl. MS. It is also in Archbishop Sancroft's MS., Tann. 465, p. 197; and was published as a broad-sheet ballad. A copy of that kind is printed in the "British Bibliographer," vol. ii. p. 181.

III.

Fill his big mind
With gallant wind
Of insolent applause;
Let him not fear the curbing laws,
  Nor king, nor people's frown;
But dream of something like a crown,
Then, climbing upwards, tumble down.

IV.

Let him appear
In his bright sphere
Like Cynthia in her pride,
With starlike troops on every side;
  For number and clear light
Such as may soon o'erwhelm him quite,
And blind them both in one dead night.

V.

Welcome, sad Night,
Grief's sole delight,
Thy mourning best agrees
With honour's funeral obsequies.
  In Thetis' lap he lies,
Mantled with soft securities,
Whose too much sunlight dims his eyes.

VI.

Was he too bold,
Who needs would hold
With curbing reins the Day,
And make Sol's fiery steeds obey?
  Therefore as rash was I,

o

Who with ambitious wings did fly
In Charles's Wain too loftily.

VII.

I fall, I fall!
Whom shall I call?
Alas! shall I be heard
Who now am neither loved nor feared?
You, who have vowed the ground
To kiss where my blest steps were found,
Come, catch me at my last rebound!

VIII.

How each admires
Heaven's twinkling fires,
Whilst from their glorious seat
Their influence gives light and heat;
But O how few there are,
Though danger from the act be far,
Will run to catch a falling star!

IX.

O were't our fate
To imitate
Those lights whose pallidness
Argues no inward guiltiness!
Their course is one way bent;
Which is the cause there's no dissent
In Heaven's High Court of Parliament.

XXXVII.

MAJESTY IN MISERY;

OR, AN IMPLORATION TO THE

KING OF KINGS.[1]

("Written by his late Majesty King Charles I., during his captivity at Carisbrook Castle, 1648.")

I.

REAT Monarch of the world, from whose power springs
The potency and power of [earthly] kings,
Record the royal woe my suffering sings;

II.

And teach my tongue, that ever did confine
Its faculties in truth's seraphic line,
To track the treasons of Thy foes and mine.

III.

Nature and law, by Thy divine decree,—
The only root of righteous royalty,—
With this dim diadem invested me;

[1] Burnet's "Memoirs of the Dukes of Hamilton," 1677, pp. 381-3, as "a copy of verses written by his Majesty in his captivity, which a very worthy gentleman, who had the honour of waiting on him then, and was much trusted by him, copied out from the original; who avoucheth it to be a true copy."

IV.

With it the sacred sceptre, purple robe,
The holy unction and the royal globe;
Yet am I levelled with the life of Job.

V.

The fiercest furies, that do daily tread
Upon my grief, my grey discrowned head,
Are those that owe my bounty for their bread.

VI.

They raise a war, and christen it The Cause;
Whilst sacrilegious hands have best applause,
Plunder and murder are the kingdom's laws.

VII.

Tyranny bears the title of taxation;
Revenge and robbery are reformation;
Oppression gains the name of sequestration.

VIII.

My loyal subjects, who, in this bad season,
Attend me by the law of God and reason,
They dare impeach, and punish for high treason.

IX.

Next at the clergy do their furies frown;
Pious episcopacy must go down;
They will destroy the crosier and the crown.

X.

Churchmen are chained, and schismatics are freed;
Mechanics preach, and holy fathers bleed;
The crown is crucified with the creed.

XI.

The Church of England doth all faction foster;
The pulpit is usurped by each impostor;
Extempore excludes the *Paternoster*.

XII.

The Presbyter and Independent seed
Springs with broad blades; to make religion bleed,
Herod and Pontius Pilate are agreed.

XIII.

The corner stone's misplaced by every pavior:
With such a bloody method and behaviour
Their ancestors did crucify our Saviour.

XIV.

My royal consort, from whose fruitful womb
So many princes legally have come,
Is forced in pilgrimage to seek a tomb.

XV.

Great Britain's heir is forced into France,
Whilst on his father's head his foes advance:
Poor child! he weeps out his inheritance.

XVI.

With my own power my majesty they wound;
In the king's name the king himself's uncrowned;
So doth the dust destroy the diamond.

XVII.

With propositions daily they enchant
My people's ears, such as do reason daunt,
And the Almighty will not let me grant.

XVIII.

They promise to erect my royal stem,
To make me great, to advance my diadem,
If I will first fall down and worship them;

XIX.

But for refusal they devour my thrones,
Distress my children and destroy my bones:
I fear they'll force me to make bread of stones.

XX.

My life they prize at such a slender rate,
That in my absence they draw bills of hate,
To prove the king a traitor to the state.

XXI.

Felons obtain more privilege than I :
They are allowed to answer ere they die ;
'Tis death for me to ask the reason, Why.

XXII.

But, sacred Saviour ! with Thy words I woo
Thee to forgive, and not be bitter to
Such as, Thou knowest, do not know what they do.

XXIII.

For since they from their Lord are so disjointed
As to condemn those edicts He appointed,
How can they prize the power of His anointed ?

XXIV.

Augment my patience ; nullify my hate ;
Preserve my issue, and inspire my mate ;
Yet, though we perish, bless this Church and State !
Vota dabunt quæ bella negarunt.

XXXVIII.

THE LIBERTY OF THE IMPRISONED ROYALIST.[1]

(By Sir Roger l'Estrange.)

I.

BEAT on, proud billows! Boreas, blow!
 Swell, curled waves, high as Jove's
  roof!
 Your incivility shall know
That innocence is tempest-proof.
Though surly Nereus frown, my thoughts are calm ;
Then strike, Affliction, for thy wounds are balm.

II.

 That which the world miscalls a gaol,
  A private closet is to me,
 Whilst a good conscience is my bail,
  And innocence my liberty.
Locks, bars, walls, leanness, though together met,
Make me no prisoner, but an anchoret.

[1] From an original 4to edition in my possession, compared with a copy in Lloyd's " Memoirs," 1668, p. 96; both anonymous. Lloyd calls the verses " the generous expressions of a worthy personage that suffered deeply in those times, and enjoys only the conscience of having so suffered in these." The piece was assigned to Lord Capel in the " Gentleman's Magazine " for Feb. 1757; but is given to L'Estrange in a Harl. MS. that belonged to Lord Capel himself; see Park's Walpole, " Royal and Noble Authors," vol. iii. p. 35. Other copies are mentioned by Percy.

III.

I, whilst I wished to be retired,
    Into this private room was turned;
As if their wisdoms had conspired
    A salamander should be burned;
And like a sophy who would drown a fish,
I am condemned to suffer what I wish.

IV.

The Cynic hugs his poverty,
    The pelican her wilderness;
And 'tis the Indian's pride to be
    Naked on frozen Caucasus.
Contentment cannot smart; Stoics, we see,
Make torments easy by their apathy.

V.

These manacles upon my arm
    I as my mistress' favours wear;
And then, to keep my ancles warm,
    I have some iron shackles there:
These walls are but my garrison; this cell,
Which men call gaol, doth prove my citadel.

VI.

So he that struck at Jason's life,
    Thinking he had his purpose sure,
By a malicious friendly knife
    Did only wound him to a cure.
Malice, I see, wants wit; for what is meant
Mischief, oft-times proves favour in the event.

VII.

Here sin for want of food doth starve,
    Where tempting objects are not seen;
And these strong walls do only serve
    To keep vice out, not let sin in.
Malice of late's grown charitable sure;
I'm not committed, but I'm kept secure.

VIII.

I'm in this cabinet locked up,
    As some high-prized margarite;
And, like some great Mogul or Pope,
    Am cloistered up from public sight.
Retiredness is a point of majesty;
And thus, proud Sultan, I'm as great as thee!

IX.

When once my prince affliction hath,
    Prosperity doth treason seem;
And then to smooth so rough a path,
    I can learn patience too from him.
Now not to suffer shows no loyal heart;
When kings want ease, subjects must learn to smart.

X.

What though I cannot see my king,—
    Either in's person, or—his coin;
Yet contemplation is a thing
    Which renders what I have not mine:
My king from me what adamant can part?
Whom I do wear engraven on my heart.

XI.

My soul is free as ambient air,
    Although my baser parts be mew'd ;
Whilst loyal thoughts do still repair
    To company my solitude ;
And though rebellion may my body bind,
My king can only captivate my mind.

XII.

Have you not seen the nightingale
    A pilgrim cooped into a cage,
And heard her tell her wonted tale,
    In that her narrow hermitage ?
Even then her charming melody doth prove
That all her bars are trees, her cage a grove.

XIII.

I am the bird whom they combine
    Thus to deprive of liberty ;
But though they do my corps confine,
    Yet, maugre hate, my soul is free.
And though I'm mew'd, yet I can chirp and sing,
Disgrace to rebels, glory to my king !

XXXIX.

AN EXCELLENT NEW BALLAD.

TO THE TUNE OF "I'LL NEVER LOVE THEE MORE."[1]

(By James, Marquis of Montrose. Born
1612; died 1650.)

I.

M Y dear and only love, I pray
    That little world of thee
Be governed by no other sway
    Than purest monarchy;
For if confusion have a part,
    Which virtuous souls abhor,
And hold a *synod* in thine heart,
    I'll never love thee more.

II.

As Alexander I will reign,
    And I will reign alone;
My thoughts did evermore disdain
    A rival on my throne.
He either fears his fate too much,
    Or his deserts are small,
That dares not put it to the touch,
    To gain or lose it all.

[1] Napier's "Memoirs of Montrose," 1856, Appendix, p.
xxxiv. from two old copies, and with a second part which
is probably older than Montrose; see Chappell's "Popular
Music of the Olden Time," second edition, p. 379. I have
introduced one or two small corrections from other copies.

III.

But I will reign and govern still,
  And always give the law,
And have each subject at my will,
  And all to stand in awe;
But 'gainst my batteries if I find
  Thou kick, or vex me sore,
As that thou set me up a blind,
  I'll never love thee more.

IV.

And in the empire of thine heart,
  Where I should solely be,
If others do pretend a part,
  Or dare to vie with me,
Or if *committees* thou erect,
  And go on such a score,
I'll laugh and sing at thy neglect,
  And never love thee more.

V.

But if thou wilt prove faithful, then,
  And constant of thy word,
I'll make thee glorious by my pen,
  And famous by my sword;
I'll serve thee in such noble ways
  Was never heard before;
I'll crown and deck thee all with bays,
  And love thee more and more.

XL.

UNHAPPY IS THE MAN.[1]

(By James, Marquis of Montrose.)

UNHAPPY is the man
    In whose breast is confined
The sorrows and distresses all
    Of an afflicted mind.

The extremity is great:
He dies if he conceal,—
The world's so void of secret friends,—
    Betrayed if he reveal.

Then break, afflicted heart!
And live not in these days,
When all prove merchants of their faith,—
    None trusts what other says.

For when the sun doth shine,
Then shadows do appear;
But when the sun doth hide his face
    They with the sun retire.

Some friends as shadows are,
And fortune as the sun;
They never proffer any help,
    Till fortune hath begun;

[1] Reprinted from Watson's " Scots' Poems." 1706-11, by Park, Walpole's " R. and N. A.," vol v. p. 106, and Napier, " Life of Montrose," 1856, Appendix, p. xli., and p. 372.

But if, in any case,
Fortune shall first decay,
Then they, as shadows of the sun,
With fortune run away.

XLI.

MOTTOES AND EJACULATIONS.

BY JAMES, MARQUIS OF MONTROSE.

I.

ON CÆSAR'S COMMENTARIES.[1]

HOUGH Cæsar's paragon I cannot be,
Yet shall I soar in thoughts as high as he.

II.

ON QUINTUS CURTIUS.[1]

S Philip's noble son did still disdain
All but the dear applause of merited
fame,
And nothing harboured in that lofty brain,
But how to conquer an eternal name,
So great attempts, heroic ventures, shall
Advance my fortune or renown my fall.

[1] Hawthornden MSS. vol. viii. Printed by Laing and Napier.

III.

UPON THE DEATH OF KING CHARLES I.[1]

GREAT, good, and just! could I but rate
    My griefs and thy too rigid fate,
    I'd weep the world to such a strain,
As it should deluge once again.
But since thy loud-tongued blood demands supplies
More from Briareus' hands than Argus' eyes,
I'll sing thy obsequies with trumpet sounds,
And write thy epitaph with blood and wounds.

MONTROSE.

IV.[2]

LET them bestow on every airt a limb;
    Then open all my veins, that I may swim
    To Thee, my Maker, in that crimson lake;
Then place my par-boiled head upon a stake;
Scatter my ashes; strew them in the air:
Lord! since Thou know'st where all these atoms are,
I'm hopeful Thou'lt recover once my dust,
And confident Thou'lt raise me with the just!

[1] In "Monumentum Regale," 1649, p. 45, as "written with the point of his sword." In "The History of the King's Majesty's affairs in Scotland," &c., 1649, at the end of the Preface, with the same note. So also in Lloyd's "Memoirs," 1668, p. 223, cf. p. 641; and in Winstanley's "England's Worthies," 1684, p. 533. For the true account see Napier's "Memoirs of Montrose," 1856, Appendix, pp. xxvii-ix.; cf. p. 693.

[2] Napier's "Memoirs of Montrose," 1856, p. 796, and App., p. xxx.

NOTES.

NOTES ON PART I.

RALEIGH'S POEMS.

THOUGH the striking vicissitudes of Raleigh's life have made it a favourite theme for biographers, no research has been expended on his poems since the days of Oldys (1736), unless I may venture to claim an exception for a little volume published by myself in 1845. Oldys mentioned about seventeen different pieces; but his references long remained neglected and unverified. In Birch's edition of " Raleigh's Minor Works " (1751), only nine of his poems were included;[1] and when Sir E. Brydges published, in 1813-4, the thin quarto volume which he called, "The Poems of Sir Walter Raleigh, *now first collected*," he made no attempt to exhaust the materials which Oldys had gathered; but swelled out Birch's nine to twenty-eight, by accepting two questionable pieces from Cayley, and appropriating seventeen poems—thirteen from "England's Helicon," and four from " Reliquiæ Wottonianæ," —on the worthless evidence of the signature

---

[1] Namely, in this volume, Part I., Nos. I. IV. V. VI. XIV. XVI. XVII. XXII. and XXIII. 8.

"Ignoto."[1] Not one of these nineteen additions
has been hitherto authenticated by conclusive
evidence.   I have allowed three to remain, with
some misgivings; for they rest on the weakest
proofs of any poems which are still included in
Part I.[2]   The remaining sixteen may be rejected
altogether from the list of Raleigh's writings.   In
fact, six at least can be proved to be the work of
other writers; and the authorship of the rest is
quite unknown.

The Oxford editors of 1829 accepted Brydges'
collection with only one unexplained omission, and
annexed eleven "additional poems," most of which
had been pointed out by Oldys nearly a century
before.   Two of these additions were mere attacks
on Raleigh.[3]   The whole set, however, is retained
in some form in the present volume;[4] and, in seve-
ral instances, the evidence which has been dis-
covered is of the highest order.   But this whole-
sale adoption of so uncritical a collection as that
of Brydges into the only general edition of Ra-
leigh's works has proved to be a real literary mis-

[1] The fact that this signature meant simply what it says,
that an author was unknown to the original editor or printer,
was established in my former volume (Introd. pp. xxix-
xxxiv).   A complete list of all the pieces ascribed to Ra-
leigh which I have rejected will be found in this volume
(Appendix to Introd. B.), and several of them are now
printed under other heads, as there referred to.

[2] Namely, Nos. xxvi. and xxvii. on the singularly weak
evidence of the obliterated signature in " England's Helicon ;"
and No. xxix. on the authority of the " London Magazine."

[3] See Appendix to the Introduction A, No. iii. 1, and
iv. 2.

[4] See Part I. Nos. ii. viii. ix. x. xi., two fragments in
No. xxiii., and No. xxviii., together with the Appendix to
the Introduction, as above.

fortune. Even the most careful of Raleigh's biographers have been misled by it into illustrating his supposed emotions from verses to which he has not the shadow of a claim.

The additions made to Raleigh's Poems in the present publication amount to more than twice as much as I have been able to retain from former editors.[1] The most important of these fresh materials is the " Continuation of Cynthia," No. xx., which is now first published from the Hatfield MSS. The " Petition to Queen Anne of Denmark," No. xxi., was first printed from the Hawthornden MSS., by Mr. D. Laing, in 1828-32. A few smaller pieces have been drawn direct from other MS. sources.[2] In the case of two well-known little poems, which were published anonymously, or under other names, during Raleigh's lifetime (Nos. vii. and xxv.), the discovery of some printed evidence in his favour is due to Mr. J. Payne Collier. The lines addressed to Gorges and Lithgow (Nos. xix. and xxx.), have frequently been mentioned; but it has been a singular oversight in editors to omit poems so accessible, and so well authenticated, as Nos. iii. and xv., which were assigned to Raleigh as early as 1591 and 1602, or to neglect the obvious duty of collecting the Metrical Translations (No. xxiv. 1-69), which occur throughout the " History of the World."

    i. p. 3. *Walter Rawely of the Middle Temple.*

---

[1] Of about 1557 lines of verse included in Part I. the nine poems in Birch make 254; the three pieces retained from Brydges' additions, 80; and the Oxford additions retained, 136; in all, 470. My additions amount altogether to about 1087 verses.

[2] *e. g.* Nos. xii. xiii. xviii. and two or three fragments in No. xxiii.

As Raleigh declared on his trial, with a strong asseveration, that he had never "read a word of the law or statute before" he "was prisoner in the Tower" (Oldys' "Life of Raleigh," p. ccxliii.), we must suppose that he was merely a resident in the Temple for some short time after his return from France in 1576. There is no good reason for doubting that he wrote the verses, to which there is no other claimant. The point is discussed by all his biographers. Oldys believed that he had discovered " the links, if not the perfect chain, of some acquaintance between" Raleigh and Gascoigne (" Life," p. xi.).

III. p. 5. *Epitaph on Sir Philip Sidney.* Raleigh's claim to this poem was substantiated from Malone's papers in 1821 (" Shakespeare," by Boswell, ii. 580), and in my former volume of 1845 (pp. xxxvii.-viii.). It cannot be doubted that Sir John Harington was alluding to the closing lines, when he wrote of " Our English Petrarch, Sir Philip Sidney, or, as Sir Walter Raleigh in his Epitaph worthily calleth him, the Scipio and the Petrarch of our time" (" Translation of Ariosto," 1591, Notes on Book xvi. p. 126). And Drummond of Hawthornden, in his character of several authors, says : " S. W. R., in an epitaph on Sidney, calleth him our English Petrarch " (" Works," ed. 1711, p. 226). The second stanza is very obscure, and if separated from the first by a full stop, as usually printed, has no construction. I take it to mean, " Yet (one may try to praise thee who is) rich in zeal, though poor in learning ; rich in care ; rich in love, which envy suppressed during thy dear life now done, and which thy death hath now doubled." In stanza 5, the king

who gave Sidney his name was Philip of Spain,
after whom many Englishmen were called, while
he was the husband of Queen Mary. The twelfth
stanza reminds us of the inscription (copied from
the French) which was formerly suspended, in
memory of Sidney, in the choir of old St.
Paul's :—

> " His body hath England, for she it bred,
> Netherlands his blood, in her defence shed ;
> The heavens have his soul ; the arts have his fame ;
> All soldiers the grief ; the world his good name."
>> Zouch's " Life of Sidney," p. 289 ; Milman's
>> " St. Paul's," p. 379.

Compare one of the epitaphs on Raleigh him-
self :—

> " Heaven hath his soul ; the world his fame ;
> The grave his corpse ; Stukeley his shame."
>> Wood's " A. O." by Bliss, ii. 244.

The Elegy on Sidney, which follows Raleigh's,
both in the " Phœnix Nest " and in Spenser's
volume — a poem of forty lines, beginning,
" Silence augmenteth grief, writing increaseth
rage "— is entitled, " Another *of the same ;*" to
which is added, in the former copy, " excellently
written by a most worthy gentleman." Raleigh's
second poem on the " Fairy Queen " (No. v.), is
also headed " Another of the same ;" but, in this
case, the phrase has generally been understood to
mean "of the same nature," rather than "ejusdem
auctoris." It was ascribed by Malone to Sir E.
Dyer on the ground of the metre (which is, how-
ever, extremely common), and by Charles Lamb
to Lord Brooke on internal evidence.

IV. p. 8. *Sonnet on the Fairy Queen.* This
noble sonnet is alone sufficient to place Raleigh
in the rank of those few original writers who can

introduce and perpetuate a new type in a litera-
ture; a type distinct from the "visions" which
Spenser translated.   The highest tribute which it
has received is the imitation of Milton :—

" Methought I saw my late espoused saint."

But Mr. Todd quotes a sonnet, printed as early as
1594, beginning :—

" Methought I saw upon Matilda's tomb."

Waldron gives another, signed "E. S.," which was
printed in 1612 :—

" Methought I saw in dead of silent night."

And the echo is still repeated by poets nearer our
own times.

" Methought I saw the footsteps of a throne."
        Wordsworth, " Miscellaneous Sonnets."

" Methought I saw a face divinely fair,
    With nought of earthly passion."
            " Lyra Apost." No. XCII.

" Methought there was around me a strange light."
        Williams, " Thoughts in Past Years," No. LV. &c.

v. p. 9.   *Another of the same.*   These very in-
ferior verses illustrate the height to which flattery
of Queen Elizabeth was carried.   It was she to
whom Spenser's poem was dedicated.   She there-
fore is the "virtue" and "beauty," which are
treated as the poet's model and appeal.   Compare
No. XXVI. p. 77.

v. p. 9, line 2.   *Philumena.*   Compare the Hat-
field MS., No. XX., p. 33, line 12 ;

"Nor Philomen recounts her direful moan."

In Gascoigne's " Complaint of Philomene," 1576,
he appears to write *Philomene* when he needs
three syllables, and *Philomela* for four.

VI. p. 11.   *Reply to Marlowe.*   The external evi-
dence that Raleigh wrote this poem is confined to

Izaak Walton ; whose assertion, however, appears
to be sufficient in the absence of any more likely
claimant. Few, I think, will agree with a modern
writer, who assigns the whole to Shakespeare,
to whom the first stanza only was ascribed in
the " Passionate Pilgrim," 1599. The statement
of Ellis, which has been constantly repeated, that
the word " Ignoto " was pasted over the original
signature " W. R." in " England's Helicon," is
an absolute mistake, arising from a confusion
with some other changes in that volume (see
here, Nos. xxvi. and xxvii.). I have examined
several copies of the original edition, and have
not found a single trace of any other signature
to this particular poem but " Ignoto;" nor is any
author's name supplied in F. Davison's " Cata-
logue of the Poems contained in England's
Helicon," in Harl. MS. 280. This disposes of
the suggestion that Walton assigned the piece
to Raleigh merely because he used " a copy in
which the alteration had not been made." In the
second edition of the " Angler," Walton inserted,
apparently from a contemporary broad-sheet (see
the " Roxburghe Collection of Ballads," i., 205,
B. M.), the following verses, as in each case the
last but one in the poem—

Marlowe. " Thy silver dishes, for thy meat,
As precious as the Gods do eat,
Shall on an ivory table be
Prepared each day for thee and me.

Raleigh. " What should we talk of dainties, then,—
Of better meat than's fit for men?
These are but vain ; that's only good,
Which God hath blest, and sent for food."

Full information on various readings, references,
and imitations may be found in Sir H. Nicolas's

ed. of Walton's " Angler," pp. 115-120 ; in
Chappell's " Popular Music of the Olden Time,"
pp. 213-215 ; and in my former volume on the
" Poems of Wotton and Raleigh," 1845, pp. 125-9,
and p. 136.

VII. p. 12. *Like Hermit Poor.* In this case
also a large store of early allusions may be found
in Nicolas's ed. of Walton's "Angler," pp. 159-
161 ; repeated with some additions in Rimbault's
" Songs and Ballads from Old Music Books,"
p. 98. Attention was first called to Raleigh's
claim by Mr. Collier, " Bibl. Cat.," ii. 223. The
lines seem, however, to have been condensed from
an earlier piece by Thomas Lodge. The various
readings are unusually numerous.

VIII. IX. X. pp. 13-15. *Poems from " Le Prince
d'Amour,"* 1660. As that small volume was pub-
lished under no particular authority, forty-two
years after Raleigh's death, the evidence of the
signature " W. R.," which it affixes to each of
these three poems, would have seemed very weak
but for the decisive discovery that Raleigh him-
self quotes a line from one of them as his own
in the Hatfield MS., above, p. 36 ;

"Of all which past, the sorrow only stays."

Compare "Hist. of the World," I. ii. 5 ; in the
last stage of life " We find by dear and lament-
able experience, and by the loss which can never
be repaired, that of all our vain passions and
affections past, the sorrow only abideth." The
expression at the end of the same piece, " My for-
tune's fold," was used by Raleigh of his estate at
Sherborne : " I am myself here at Sherborne, in
my *fortune's fold*" (to R. Cecil, May 10, 1593 ; Ed-
wards, ii. 80). No. VIII. then, being unquestionably

Raleigh's, an editor who has proved right in one point may claim our confidence for the other two pieces also. It will be seen that for each of these poems much older anonymous copies have been found. In the first line of No. x., the last word should, apparently, be "smart."

xi. p. 16. *Fain would I, but I dare not.* As the initials "W. R." appear to have been added in the Rawlinson MS. by a later hand, it is possible that they rest on mere conjecture, suggested by the well-known line ascribed by Fuller to Raleigh; No. xxiii., 1. The MSS. vary throughout the piece between "whereas" and "whenas." I believe the latter word, which is frequent in Spenser, Herrick, &c., to be correct.

xiii. p. 19. *On the Cards and Dice.* A shorter copy of these verses is still in use as a Christmas riddle. The double meaning will be easily traced all through. The day fixed in the first line probably refers to the licence which prevailed between Christmas and Twelfth Day. The fifth line means that many purses shall be emptied of their *crosses—i.e.,* coin. But it would make a better antithesis with the next line to read, "*no* end of crosses "—*i.e.,* gains. The game is supposed to be continued till cock-crowing, which gives the key to the last two lines.

xiv. p. 20. *The Silent Lover.* While the evidence in Raleigh's favour is in this case strong and general, what is alleged for three other writers is in each instance isolated and weak. In behalf of Lord Pembroke—though he has found one modern supporter—no proof exists but the fact that the piece is assigned to him in the notoriously untrustworthy collection which was edited in 1660 by the younger Dr. Donne. Aytoun's claim depends on a MS. used in an edition of his poems published at Edinburgh in 1844, the editor of which believed the piece to have been " never before printed " (p. 129). The third claim rests solely on the unsupported witness of MS. Ashm., 781, p. 143, where an imperfect copy is signed " Lo. Walden." Mr. Collier suggests that this claim arose from a confusion with Raleigh's own title, " Lord Warden of the Stannaries ;" but I doubt whether that title would have been used alone. It is enough to say that one MS. could not outweigh the authority of several, unless it possessed some direct or unusual authority. The last stanza but one, which has been ascribed to so late a writer as Lord Chesterfield, was quoted in 1652, in the dedication to a play of Fletcher's, as written by " an ingenious person of quality " (Dyce's edition, vol. viii. p. 106). Several copies omit (perhaps properly) the first six lines.

XVI. p. 23. *The Lie.* For a long time Raleigh's claim to this poem seemed unusually doubtful ; it is now established at least as conclusively as in the case of any of his poems. We have the direct testimony of two contemporary MSS., and the still stronger evidence of at least two contemporary answers, written during Raleigh's lifetime, and reproaching him with the poem by name or implication.[1] An untraced and unauthorized story, that he wrote the poem the night

---

[1] See them in Appendix to the Introduction, A. No. iv. For various readings and other details I must refer to my former volume, pp. 89-103. I had previously stated the chief points of the evidence in the " British Critic " for April 1842, pp. 344-9.

before his death, is contradicted by the dates—it was printed ten years before that time, in 1608; and it can be found in MSS. more than ten years earlier still, in 1596, 1595, or 1593.[1] But the question of the authorship is not touched by the refutation of the legend, when so many independent witnesses assert the one without the other. There are five other claimants, but not one with a case that will bear the slightest examination. For the claim of Richard Edwards we are indebted to a mere mistake of Ellis's; for that of F. Davison to a freak of Ritson's; that of Lord Essex is only known from the correspondence of Percy, who did not believe it; and those of Sylvester and Lord Pembroke are sufficiently refuted by the mutilated character of the copies which were printed among their posthumous writings.

XVII. p. 27. *The Pilgrimage.* We may perhaps account for the more strange and startling metaphors in this striking poem, by dating it during Raleigh's interval of suspense in 1603, after his condemnation and before his reprieve, when the smart of Coke's coarse cross-examination had not passed away. To explain the double meaning in

---

[1] Malone says 1595; Brydges, 1596; and Campbell, 1593. The only dated MS. which I have seen is MS. Harl. 6910, which has the date 1596 inserted on fol. 74, *verso*, between transcripts of the contents of Spenser's " Complaints," which were printed in 1591, and George Chapman's Hymns "In Noctem " and "In Cynthiam," which were printed in 1594. " The Lie " occurs among miscellaneous pieces later in the volume; and it is of course possible that they were transcribed at a later date. But the question becomes unimportant if we admit the probability that the poem was written in 1593.

page 28, line 24, note that an *angel* was also the name of a coin.

xix. p. 30. *Sir A. Gorges.* Sir Arthur Gorges was Raleigh's kinsman; had been captain of Raleigh's own ship in the island voyage, when he was wounded by his side in the landing of Fayal; and has left a history of that expedition which is of material importance in Raleigh's biography. Some verses written by him will be found in Part III., No. xxx. He is the "Alcyon" of Spenser's "Colin Clout's come home again," Collier's "Spenser," vol. v. p. 45; cf. "Daphnaida," *ib.*, 229. For further details, see Oldys' "Life of Raleigh," p. cxi., *sqq.*; Malone's "Shakespeare" by Boswell, ii. 245-8.

xx. p. 31. *Continuation of Cynthia.* Some remarks on the general drift of this obscure but important fragment will be found in the Introduction to this volume. I confine myself here to a brief comment on the text. The MS. was fully described by Mr. C. J. Stewart in his catalogue of the Cecil MSS., at Hatfield, and was mentioned by Mr. Edwards, who was prevented by an accident from printing it (see the Introduction to his "Life of Raleigh," p. xxxix). I have to thank both for their courtesy in answering my questions on the subject; and I am deeply indebted to the Marquis of Salisbury for giving me access to the MS., and to Mr. R. T. Gunton for his assistance in completing and revising the transcript, and in supplying me with minute details on the readings. The whole is in Raleigh's autograph; and the main portion is written with that "extreme precision and neatness of hand" which Mr. Edwards (vol. ii. p. 258) describes as characteristic of his

later papers; but it is obviously unfinished and
unrevised, and the construction and meaning are
often perplexed and doubtful. The spelling is
peculiar, even for that age; which may, perhaps,
be partly connected with the fact mentioned by
Aubrey ("Letters from the Bodleian," vol. ii. p.
519), that Raleigh "spake broad Devonshire to his
dying day." Thus *sun* is always "soonn" or
"soon;" *earth* is "yearth," *earthquakes* "yearth-
quakes," *air* "eayre," *evening* "yeveninge," *evil*
"yevill," *even* "yeven," and *uneven* "unyeven."
"Worlds" is twice made a dissyllable (page 38,
line 17, and page 47, line 2); as is also "worn"
in the phrase, "the sorrow-worren face" (page 49,
line 10); *sighs* are "sythes," and *sighing* "sythinge."
The termination *le* is always given broad and full:
"exampell, feebell, gentell, idell, isakells, littell,
marbell, middell, mirakells, puddells, simpell, stub-
bell, trebell," and ."unabell." This peculiarity
runs through his letters, as edited by Mr. Edwards;
where, beside the constant occurrence of the form
with adjectives ("capabell, charetabell, cumforta-
bell, forsibell, honorabell, nobell," and the like)
we find "castells, eagell, peopell, saddell, scrupell,
stabells," and "trobell." The letters also teach us
that "mich" means *much*, "nire" *near*, and "on"
one, and give many parallels to such forms as
"diing" and "fliing." Other spellings are merely
odd; as "Scinthia" (twice), and "perrellike"
(*pearl-like*). These peculiarities would have greatly
deepened the obscurity to the general reader, or I
should have preferred to print this poem in its
original dress. In style and metre, the piece is
not unlike Spenser's "Colin Clout's come home
again," which gives us the best account remaining

of the poem "Cynthia," now, I fear, irrecoverably lost. Raleigh's accents and words are often the same as Spenser's; *e.g.*, among those just mentioned, Spenser also makes "worlds" a dissyllable, and uses "on" for "one" (Collier, vol. iv. p. 295). Add the accent of "captíved," "envý," and some other words; and the familiar use of "recure" and "fordone," the former twice, the latter thrice in this one poem; and such words as "transpersant, reave, vild, intentive, brast," and several others.

Page 32, line 14. The meaning is, "As *though* the dead did unfold to the dead."

Page 33, line 5. The MS. has "frutfull," which must have been an error in writing. Compare "those healthless trees" just below; and page 41, stanza 2,

> " So far as neither fruit nor form of flower
> Stays for a witness what such branches bare."

Page 33, line 6. MS. "hands," in spite of the rhyme. So below, page 49, line 17, we have "sand" rhyming with "bands," and page 50, line 12, "blasts" with "brast."

Page 33, line 24. "Transpersant"=transpiercing; and the line means, "O piercing eyes, the bait of my affection."

Page 33, line 25. "My fancy's adamant"= magnet; compare "as iron to adamant;" "Troilus and Cressida," iii. 2.

Page 34, line 11. The MS. may be read either "affecting" or "effecting."

Page 34, stanza 5. The construction is, "When I was gone to seek new worlds," &c.

Page 35, line 22. MS. "depting," with a mark of contraction: "departing," or "depicting"? The latter (though that is not much) approaches nearest to a rhyme with "sythinge," sighing; and seems to make an easier sense.

Page 36, line 16. MS. "lymes," limbs; apparently mis-written for "lynes." The meaning is, "her memory embalmed my lines."

Page 36, stanza 6. See above, No. VIII. p. 13.

Page 39, line 17. MS. "wounders," might mean *wonders;* but apparently refers to "the tyrants that in fetters tie their *wounded* vassals," just above.

Page 40, line 6. "Fordone" = undone in Spenser, "a fordone wight;" "a virgin desolate, fordone." ("F. Q.," I. v. st. 41, and x. st. 60.) We have it twice again in this poem, page 45, line 21, and page 51, line 7, meaning, as here, departed.

Page 41, after stanza 1. Two lines in the MS. scribbled over and illegible.

Page 41, line 10. MS. "reves." To *reave* is to take away, as in *bereave.* Here used apparently for *draws*, or *derives.*

Page 42, line 3, and page 44, line 5. "Belphœbe;" see Spenser, "F. Q." III. v. st. 27, &c., and for the allegory of "Belphœbe and Timias," in which Raleigh was supposed to be concerned, see "F. Q." IV. VII; VI. v. st. 12.

Page 43, line 12. "Incarnate"=flesh-coloured; hence pink, as in carnation. See below, page 47, line 28, "the incarnate rose." The phrase "snow-driven white" must be taken together; and with the inversion we may compare page 45, line 3, "after worthless worlds"=worthless after-worlds.

Page 43, line 13. "Who" for *which;* compare "Merchant of Venice," ii. 6 (altered by Dyce);

" The first, of gold, *who* this inscription bears," &c.
" The second, silver, *which* this promise carries."

Q

Page 44, stanza 3. Three lines scribbled over and illegible. They completed the stanza of which the fourth line only is left; the middle line apparently ending with "abydinge." On this page I have used the modern forms, "forepast" and "forethought." " Forthought" (as in the MS.) would mean *repented*.

Page 48, after stanza 4. Two lines scribbled over and illegible.

Page 48, line 20. So the MS. We might have expected *un*prisoned and *un*pent.

Page 49, stanza 6. I follow the MS., but something seems wanting to complete the sense. What is required is an instance of futile labour, like seeking moisture in the Arabian desert, and the sun after sunset; or of disappointment, like the failure of Hero's light. The dots after " set" are in the MS. and it is not likely that in stanza 7, line 1, " where" and "were" have been confounded, as the MS. spells the former " wher," and the latter, as here, " weare."

Page 49, last line. " Shee *sleaps* thy death," MS.; as though, varying from the usual story, he made Hero sleep through the fatal storm, after withdrawing her light.

Page 50, line 14. "Brast "=*burst*, as in Spenser.

XXI. p. 52. *Petition to the Queen*. This petition, which has been preserved in the transcript of Drummond of Hawthornden, resembles the Hatfield fragment in the stiffness of its rhythm, and partly in its metre. In stanza 3, line 3, the MS. has " vearye," which I take to mean *very*. In stanza 5, line 2, the MS. has " descriu'd;" *i. e.*, de-*scrived* for *described*. Compare the first Sonnet which I have given from Sidney, page 138, line 4,

" thy languished grace—thy state *descries*," and "descrive" in Spenser, " F. Q." II. iii. st. 25, &c.

XXIII. p. 55. *Fragments, &c.* With No. 1, compare the piece given above from a Rawlinson MS., No. XI. p. 16.—The two riddles in No. 2 are often found apart; and that on Noel is sometimes ascribed to Queen Elizabeth.—Raleigh's claim to No. 5, the well-known epitaph on Leicester, rests solely on the evidence of the Bridgewater MSS., as reported by Mr. Collier. There are two anonymous copies among the Hawthornden MSS. at Edinburgh, the first of which was printed by Mr. Laing, and quoted in the notes to Scott's " Kenilworth:"

" Here lies a valiant warrior, who never drew a sword;
Here lies a noble courtier, who never kept his word;
Here lies the Earl of Leicester, who governed the estates,
Whom the earth could never living love, and the just heaven
    now hates."

The first line of the second copy gives a variation worth preserving: "Here lies a noble warrior, who never *stained* a sword."—Raleigh's title to No. 6, the epitaph on Salisbury, rests on the word of the biographer Shirley, who says, "which I am upon very good grounds assured to be his. King James was so much taken with the smartness of it, that he hoped the author would die before him." It is thus introduced in Osborne's " Traditional Memoirs on the Reign of King James," 1658, p. 88: " those that follow are from so smart a pen in the king's sense, that he said he hoped the author would die before him: who it was, God knows." Compare Oldys, " Life of Raleigh," p. clxxiv.—No. 7 : " My aunt Laighton " is mentioned in a well-known letter from Lord Essex to Dyer (Tytler's

" Raleigh," p. 62). A " Lady Leighton " was, I believe, one of the bedchamber-women to the Queen. A "Sir Thomas Leighton" was a governor of Guernsey; and a " Sir William" was " one of his Majesty's band of pensioners" in 1612, and is known as a writer of verses.

xxiv. pp. 58-75. These fragments of metre, which are scattered through Raleigh's " History of the World," have never been collected before. I have verified and completed the references, which were often incorrect or imperfect, and often omitted altogether. The original is nearly always prefixed in Raleigh's text, except that all the Greek passages are quoted in a Latin version. It is curious that the very first translation which we meet with in the volume is borrowed, and I have therefore omitted it; viz. book I., ch. i. § 5; Ovid, Metam. i. 5-8, from A. Golding's Ovid:

" Before the sea and land were made, and Heaven that all
      doth hide,
In all the world one only face of Nature did abide,
Which Chaos hight, a huge rude heap—"

I have not observed any other instances of the kind, though it is quite possible that some may have escaped my notice. The second quotation from Ovid stands thus in Golding (p. 46):

" Said, I am he that metes the year, that all things do be-
      hold,
By whom the earth doth all things see, the Eye of all the
      world."

The translation of Lucan, to which Raleigh prefixed a Sonnet (above, No. xix. p. 30) to oblige his relative Sir A. Gorges, is different in all the passages which Raleigh has made use of; thus:—

No. xiv. p. 61.   In Gorges, p. 141:

> " O Luxury! thou prodigue vain,
> That never canst the mean retain;
> And thou, insatiate Gluttony,
> Pampered with superfluity," &c.

No. xxxi. p. 65.   In Gorges, p. 128:

> " Cæsar small skiffs prepares and rigs,
> Composed of green willow twigs,
> And over it doth ox-hides dight,
> Wherewith to keep them staunch and tight," &c.

No. xliii. p. 68.   In Gorges, p. 93:

> " So likewise, if we credit fame,
> Phœnicians were the first had name
> The use of characters to find,
> And letters to express our mind."

But it must not be forgotten that Ben Jonson claimed a share in the great History, both for himself and for others.   The probable amount of Raleigh's obligations has been fairly stated by Oldys, exaggerated by D'Israeli, and again reduced to reasonable dimensions by Mr. Tytler, Mr. Macvey Napier, and Mr. Edwards. I have not thought it necessary to criticize the translations; but it will be observed that in No. LV. p. 72, he takes Corythus for the hero instead of the town.

XXVI. and XXVII. pp. 77-78.   The change of signature in "England's Helicon" leaves Raleigh's claims to these two poems doubtful; but it is not conclusive evidence against him, because the editor may have merely discovered that the author wished to remain concealed.

Page 78, last line.   " Sauncing bell" is frequently used for " saints' bell," *quod ad sancta vocat*. Another form found is " sacring bell," the bell announcing the elevation of the host.   " Sain " is of course *say*, as frequently in Spenser.

XXVIII. p. 80.   I think it very improbable that

Raleigh wrote this ballad. Sufficient literary references to " Walsingham Pilgrimages " will be found in Percy, and in Chappell's " Popular Music of the Olden Time," pp. 121-2.

xxix. p. 82. This is one of the replies to Wither's verses, " Shall I, wasting in despair." It seems to me quite as unlikely that Raleigh wrote this answer as that Jonson wrote another.—Gifford's " Life of Ben Jonson," p. cxlix.; Bliss's Wood, " A. O." ii. 616.

NOTES ON PART II.

THE poems contained in this Part are chiefly taken from the collection of Sir Henry Wotton's minor writings, which was first published in 1651, twelve years after the author's death, and reprinted in 1654, 1672, and 1685. The first portion consists of Sir Henry Wotton's own poems; the second of poems found among his papers. I have added nothing to this division except a few scattered pieces, which seemed to make the collection more complete.

i. p. 87. *Of a woman's heart.* Several copies insert the following couplet after line 16:

" Or w⸺ it absence that did make her strange,
  Base flower of change ? "

ii. p. 88. *Serjeant Hoskins.* John Hoskins was originally a Fellow of New College, where he graduated M.A. in 1592; but some sarcasms in which he indulged as *Terræ Filius* for that year led to his expulsion from the university. A prosperous marriage afterwards enabled him to enter at the Middle Temple, and he became a member of Parliament, where "a desperate allusion to the Sicilian Vesper" consigned him to the Tower, June 7, 1614. This date alone disposes of Wood's story, that his participation in Raleigh's imprisonment led to their intimacy, with the result that Hoskins "viewed and reviewed" the "History of the World;" for that volume, as Wood himself states, was published in April, . 1614 (A. O. ii. 238, 626). It seems clear, however, that his "company" was "much desired by ingenious men." He spent about a year in the Tower; and was afterwards successively a reader at the Temple, serjeant-at-law, a judge for Wales, and a member of the Council of the Marches. He died Aug. 27, 1638. His "book of poems, bigger than those of Dr. Donne," which was lost by his son, has never been recovered; but a good many of his epigrams can be found in the small MS. miscellanies of the time. I have printed a few in No. xxv. p. 121. Dr. Bliss printed from the Ashmole MSS. a piece of eighty lines, called "Mr. Hoskins' Dream;" edition of Wood, "A. O." ii. 627. One of the epigrams which I have given consists of lines extracted from it.

III. p. 89. *A happy life.* The third stanza seems to be corrupt, but the reading given here is at all events intelligible; "Nor envies any whom vice doth raise." The copy found in Ben Jonson's handwriting sanctions this punctuation, reading "Or vice; who never understood." The text in "Rel. Wotton." leaves it without construction, reading "Nor vice hath ever understood; How deepest," &c. Mr. Dyce reads: "Nor vice; hath ever understood," &c.

VII. p. 95. *On the Queen of Bohemia.* This sprightly poem must have been written during the short interval which elapsed after Sept. 1619, before the brief day of Elizabeth's Bohemian sovereignty was clouded. It has been a favourite theme for imitations and additions; of which three stanzas will be a sufficient specimen. The first and second are taken from Archbishop Sancroft's MS., Tann. 465, fol. 43, where they rank as fourth and sixth (compare a somewhat similar copy in the "Topographer," i. 421); the third, in which the metre is altogether altered, is taken from the end of the copy in the Aberdeen "Cantus." It has found its way, with some variations, among Montrose's poems (Napier's "Life of Montrose," 1856, Appendix, p. xl).

" You rubies that do gems adorn,
    And sapphires with your azure hue,
Like to the skies or blushing morn;
    How pale's your brightness in our view,
    When diamonds are mixed with you?

" The rose, the violet, all the spring,
    Unto her breath for sweetness run;
The diamond's darkened in the ring;
    If she appear, the moon's undone,
    As in the presence of the sun.

" Should little streams command great seas,
Or little ants the stinging bees?
Should little birds with eagles soar,
Or little beasts with lions roar?
No, no, not so, it is not meet
The head should stoop down to the feet."

VIII. p. 96. Sir Albertus Morton was Wotton's nephew, and had been his secretary at Venice. He was frequently employed by King James on foreign affairs, was knighted by him in 1617, and died secretary of state in 1625. Sir Henry never mentions him without adding some expressions of affectionate regard.

IX. p. 98. Sir A. Morton's wife was Elizabeth, daughter of Sir Edward Apsley, of Thakeham, Sussex; was married Jan. 13, 1624, and died *s. p.* in 1627.

X. p. 98. The allusion in the first stanza is to the planet which was said to be visible at noon-day at the birth of Charles II., May 29, 1630. It was commemorated at the time, more or less directly, by Wotton, King, Corbet, Cleveland, and Herrick; and after the restoration, by Cowley and Waller. The figure of a star is found on some of the medals of Charles II.

XI. p. 99. Sir H. Wotton wrote a Latin tract (afterwards inserted in " Rel. Wotton.") upon the same occasion, with the title, " Ad Regem è Scotiâ reducem Henrici Wottonii plausus et vota, MDCXXXIII." It was reprinted in various forms, both in Latin and English.

XIII. p. 103, line 1. *valing ebbs—i. e.* failing, or retiring. Near the end, *vade* is fade, depart.

XV. p. 106. *Howell's Dodona's Grove.* This flattering estimate of Howell's allegory has not been ratified. Mr. Hallam summarily calls it "an entire failure." The reference in line 4 is doubtless to the well-known " Argenis " of John Barclay, and the " Advices from Parnassus " of Trajan Boccalini.

XVII. p. 109. I have transferred this well-known piece from the "Complete Angler," as particularly suitable in style and subject, if not in authorship, to have formed part of the collection in " Rel. Wotton."

Page 110, line 6. " Mind," *i. e.* mine, as it is

spelt in Sancroft's MS. In some copies the line begins, "Dig *out* the bowels," which may be correct.

Page 110, line 20. An angel was a piece of money worth ten shillings (see above, p. 28, line 24, and note). To "vie angels" is to stake or hazard coins against an antagonist, who may "re-vie" if he is able, by putting down a larger sum.

Page.111, line 7. In Sancroft's MS. these lines stand thus:

> " Here dwell no heating loves, no palsy fears,
> No short joys purchased with eternal tears :
> Here will I sit, and sigh my hot youth's folly," &c.

XVIII. p. 111, line 3. Observe that the word "world's" is here a dissyllable, as it occurs twice in the Hatfield MS. (see above, p. 38, line 17, and p. 47, line 2.)

XIX. p. 112. Dr. Samuel Brooke, the intimate friend of Dr. Donne, was a member of Trinity College, Cambridge, where he graduated as M.A. in 1604, and as D.D. in 1615. He was successively Divinity Professor of Gresham College, Rector of St. Margaret's, Lothbury, Master of Trinity, and Archdeacon of Coventry; and died in 1631. His brother, Christopher Brooke, was better known as an English poet. He is probably the author of "The Ghost of Richard the Third," 1614, a poem which was republished by the Shakespeare Society. References to both brothers may be found among the poems of Donne, Crashaw, and William Browne.

XX. p. 114. Chidiock Tychbourne, of Southampton, was executed, with Ballard and Babington, in 1586. The reply to his verses, which I copied many years ago from a contemporary MS., has been preserved in rather an imperfect form. In line 4, the MS. reads, "Thy hope in hurt *as wasted*," the writer's eye having caught the line above; in line 11, there is an evident omission, which I have attempted to supply; in line 16, the MS. reads, " hadst ne'er been *born;*" and, in the last line, it makes an unnecessary insertion,— "Which, O unhappy *man*," &c. I am doubtful about the reading of one or two other words. "Lewdly," in line 14, means mistakenly, ignorantly.

XXI. p. 116. The repetition of "thoughts" in line 4 appears to be an error; but it stands so in all the editions I have used. The shortness of line 5 in the old editions is not countenanced by the form of the other stanzas. The word which I have supplied is found only in some modern copies. This piece is followed in " Rel. Wotton." by Raleigh's lines, " Even such is time," which have been given already in Part I. No. XXII. p. 54.

XXII. p. 117. Though there is no reason to doubt that Bacon wrote these verses, his claim does not seem to have been commonly known ; for it will be seen that his name was an after-insertion in many of the MS. copies, as well as in "Rel. Wotton." The lines bear some resemblance to a well-known epigram ascribed to Posidippus, which had been very frequently translated ; *e. g.* in Tottel's " Songs and Sonnets," 1557 ; in Puttenham's " Art of Poesy," 1589 ; by Sir John Beaumont, and by others. Possibly from this circumstance, the last line frequently occurs in almost exactly the same shape among the minor poems of the time ; *e. g.* Bacon, as here :

> " What then remains, but that we still should cry
> For being born, and, being born, to die? "

Drummond of Hawthornden, "Works," 1711;
Poems, p. 44:

> " Who would not one of those two offers try,—
> Not to be born, or, being born, to die?"

Bishop King, "Poems," &c. 1657, p. 145:

> " At least with that Greek sage still make us cry,
> Not to be born, or, being born, to die."

The mythical author of the phrase was Silenus,
who is said to have bestowed it on his captor,
King Midas.

xxv. p. 121, No. 1.   The son of Hoskins who is
generally mentioned was called *Benedict* or *Bennet.*
Hence it is very probable that Hoskins wrote " My
little *Ben*," &c. which is the reading of a Rawlin-
son MS.

NOTES ON PART III.

IT will save repetition to note here, that
the old editions of the early poetical mis-
cellanies, by which I have rectified the
text of extracts, are as follows :—Tottel's " Songs
and Sonnets," those of 1557 and 1585; " The Para-
dise of Dainty Devices " (first published in 1576),
those of 1580 and 1596; " The Phœnix Nest,"
1593; " England's Helicon," the first edition,
1600; and Davison's " Poetical Rhapsody " (first
published in 1602), generally the fourth edition,
1621.   But in giving mere lists of first lines, I
have referred by page to the reprints of Park,
Brydges, &c., as most likely to be commonly ac-
cessible; and I have availed myself, in one or two

instances, which are duly acknowledged, of further information contained in Mr. Collier's recent re-prints.

I. p. 125. The seventh line of this piece, "As lead to grave in marble stone," means, "as *for* lead *to* engrave," &c.; that is, it is as hard for my song to pierce her heart, as for the soft metal to cut letters on the hard marble. In line 24, "unquit" means "unrequited, unpunished." In line 26, as again in line 31, "may chance thee lie," means, "*it* may chance *for* thee to lie," &c. The Harington MS. destroys the sense by reading, "*Per-*chance *they* lie withered and old."

II. p. 127. The copy ascribed to John Heywood is printed at length by Park in his notes to Walpole, "R. and N. A." vol. i. p. 80. It can scarcely be doubted that Heywood has simply laid hands on a popular poem for purposes of flattery, and utterly destroyed its beauty in the process. His copy closes thus :—

> " This worthy lady, too, bewray;
>   A king's daughter was she,
> Of whom John Heywood list to say
>   In such worthy degree.

> " And Mary was her name, weet ye,
>   With these graces endued;
> At eighteen years so flourished she:
>   So doth his mean conclude."

The readings "roscal" (st. 8, line 1), "lively" (*ib.* line 4), and "honesty" (st. 11, line 3), are from the old copies; instead of "roseate," "lovely," and "modesty," as given in some modern texts.

III.—VI. pp. 129-134. *Thomas, Lord Vaux.* I have here selected four pieces out of sixteen, which are ascribed to this nobleman; two of them printed among the uncertain authors in Tottel's " Songs and Sonnets," and fourteen in " The Paradise of

Dainty Devices." The following are the first lines
of the other twelve, arranged alphabetically :—

5. " How can the tree but waste and wither
away."—P. of D. D., p. 64; "L. Vaux." An anony-
mous copy in Harl. MS. 6910, fol. 168, *verso* ; and
another printed from a Music-Book of 1596 by
Mr. Collier, " Lyrical Poems," &c. p. 31.

6. " If ever man had love too dearly bought."—
P. of D. D., p. 73; "L. V."

7. " I loathe that I did love."—Tottel, anon.
Ascribed to Lord Vaux " in time of the noble
Queen Mary," in Harl. MS. 1703, fol. 100. See
more on this poem in Percy, Warton (iii. 54, ed.
Park), and the Commentators on Hamlet.

8. " Like as the hart that lifteth up his ears."—
P. of D. D., p. 81; " L. Vaux."

9. " Mistrust misdeems amiss, whereby dis-
pleasure grows."—P. of D. D., p. 82: " L. V."

10. " The day delayed of that I most do wish."
—P. of D. D., p. 10; " L. Vaux."

11. " To counsel my estate abandoned to the
spoil."—P. of D. D., p. 81; " L. Vaux."

12. " What doom is this, I fain would know."—
P. of D. D., p. 72; " L. V."

13. " What grieves my bones and makes my
body faint?"—P. of D. D., p. 3; " L. Vaux."

14. " When Cupid scaled first the fort."—Tottel,
anon. Quoted, with a wrong Christian name, by
Puttenham, A. P. 1589, p. 200, as by " the Lord
Nicholas Vaux, a noble gentleman, and much de-
lighted in vulgar making," &c. A copy in Harl.
MS. 6910, fol. 175. See also Warton (iii. 57),
Percy, and Ellis.

15. " When I behold the bier, my last and post-
ing horse."—P. of D. D., p. 103; " L. Vaux."

16. " Where seething sighs and sour sobs."—
P. of D. D., p. 44; "L. V." In some editions
ascribed to W. Hunnis. The fifth stanza begins,
"These hairs of age are messengers;" which forms
the first line in some modern copies.

It will be observed that at least three of the
sixteen, including two of those which I have given
at length, have been also claimed for other authors.
The same remark will apply to two other pieces,
the first lines of which I add here :—

17. " Brittle beauty, that nature made so frail."
—Found also among Lord Surrey's Poems; but
Dr. Nott is rather anxious to resign it to Lord
Vaux. See his edition of Surrey, pp. 20, 288.

18. " To seem for to revenge each wrong in
hasty wise."—P. of D. D., p. 30; "E. S." Mr.
Collier mentions that there is "early authority"
(e. g. ed. 1580) for Lord Vaux; "Bibl. Cat." i. 245.

III. p. 129. This is undoubtedly very "heavy
verse," as the author acknowledges; and it is ex-
tremely obscure. In the second stanza we may
perhaps suspect an inversion; as though the
first and third lines were nearly transposed: " If
weary woe enwrapped in the shroud my wonted
cheer, which is eclipsed, &c. (so that it) lies slain
by tongue of the unfriendly sort." (Both the old
editions used read, "If weary we.") In line 15,
all the copies I have seen read, "On that I gape
the issue," &c., for which I have conjectured,
" gage," i. e. stake.

IV. p. 130. The old reading of the first line,
" do grow," is an instance of one of the commonest
errors in Elizabethan grammar; when the verb is
made to agree with the number of the nearest
noun, even though not a nominative at all. So

in line 4, the old reading is, "*lies* hid." Compare page 78, line 9, where the old editions have, " By her the *virtue* of the stars down *slide*."

v. p. 132.　The old editions used omit " in " in the second line, and in line 3, begin " *The* most of all."　In line 21, I have followed Ellis and others in reading " Fear " for " Few."

vii. p. 135.　The smoothness and ingenuity of this piece, at so early a date, have caused some suspicions.　" If these are genuine," says Mr. Hallam, " and I know not how to dispute it, they are as polished as any written at the close of the Queen's reign."　It is confessed that there is one mistake already in the date; but Park's proposal to support a legend prefixed to them by substituting one still earlier, would only increase the marvel.　In one or two words I have followed the readings of Dr. Nott, " Surrey," p. cclxxix.

viii. p. 136.　The scattered verses ascribed to Queen Elizabeth are collected in Park's Walpole, " R. and N. A.," i. 84-109, and in Mr. Dyce's " British Poetesses," pp. 15-23.　In line 21 of this piece, " The daughter of debate" is Mary Queen of Scots.　The last couplet, as it stands in Puttenham, is imperfect.　I have supplied the deficiency from the Oxford MS.　Percy reads, "shall *quickly* poll;" Brydges, "for *lawless* joy."

ix.-x. pp. 137—141.　It is impossible to represent properly the Courtly Poets of Elizabeth without an extract from the writings of Sir Philip Sidney; in whose case I have therefore made a brief exception to the rule, which has led me generally to exclude specimens from those poets whose works have already been collected and edited.　All requisite information on the version of the Psalms ascribed to Sidney and his sister is given in Park's edition

of Walpole's "Royal and Noble Authors," vol. ii.
pp. 203-4, and in the Preface prefixed to the first
printed edition in 1823.

xi-xv. pp. 142-7. *Edward, Earl of Oxford.* To
the five pieces here ascribed to Lord Oxford, the
following sixteen may be added, making twenty-
one in all :—

6. " A crown of bays shall that man wear."—
Par. of D. D., p. 70 ; " E. O."

7. " Doth sorrow fret thy soul ? O, direful
spirit!"—Six lines in "England's Parnassus," 1600,
p. 26, reprint ; " E. of O." Also anon. with
" Astrophel and Stella," 1591.

8. " Even as the wax doth melt, or dew con-
sume away."—P. of D. D., p. 77 ; " E. O."

9. " Faction that ever dwells in court where wit
excels."—Printed with Sidney's " Astrophel and
Stella;" and reprinted in Collier's " Bibl. Cat.,"
Additions, p. ii.; " E. O." Cf. *ib.*, vol. i. p. 37.

10. " Framed in the front of forlorn hope past all
recovery."—P. of D. D., p. 24 (corrected); " E. O."

11. "I am not as I seem to be."—P. of D. D.,
p. 76 ; " E. O."

12. " If care or skill could conquer vain desire."
—P. of D. D., p. 74; " M. B.," but ascribed to Lord
Oxford in ed. 1578 (Collier), and in ed. 1580.

13. " Love is a discord and a strange divorce."
—Eighteen lines in " England's Parnassus," p.
208; " E. O."

14. " My meaning is to work what wonders
love hath wrought."—P. of D. D. p. 78; " E. O."

15. " Sitting alone upon my thought in melan-
choly mood."—" Verses made by the Earl of Ox-
ford ;" MS. Rawl. 85, fol. 11.

16. " The lively lark did stretch her wing."—

R

P. of D. D. p. 69; "E. O." MS. Rawl. 85, fol. 14, *verso.* "Earl of Oxford."

17. "The trickling tears that fall along my cheeks."—P. of D. D. p. 75; "E. O."

18. "What plague is greater than the grief of mind?"—Six lines in "England's Parnassus," p. 252; "E. of Ox." Anon. with "Astrophel and Stella."

19. "What shepherd can express."—England's Helicon, p. 87; "Earl of Oxenford."

20. "When I was fair and young, then favour graced me."—Lord Orford's Works, i. 552, "from an ancient MS. Miscellany." Also in Ellis. But in MS. Rawl. Poet. 85, fol. 1, signed "Elysabetha regina."

21. "Who taught thee first to sigh, alas! my heart."—MS. Rawl. 85, fol. 16, *verso.* "Earl of Oxenford."

XI. p. 142. The copies of this piece differ widely. That which Ellis has printed resembles the text of the Harleian MS. The following readings may be worth observing: line 6, "*pride* of May;" line 14, "*unsavoury* lovers' tears;" line 32, "*Ten* thousand times a day."

XII. p. 143. In the third line, Mr. Palgrave rightly corrected Dr. Bliss's reading, "make *me* bond," into "make *men* bond." It is "men" in the copy printed by Byrd in 1587.

XIII. p. 144. This singular poem looks like an exercise in alliteration. In line 6, "or" probably means "before;" "before I suffer wrong again."

XIV. p. 146, line 1. *Manchet* is fine bread, which is constantly, as here, contrasted with *cheat*, or coarse bread. In the "proportion for a royal dinner," in the time of Philip and Mary, the first three items are, "Fyne manchett, fyne chett, and other chett;" Gutch, "Collect. Cur." vol. ii. *init.*

" No *manchet* can so well the courtly palate please,
As that made of the meal fetched from my fertile leas;
Their finest of that kind, compared with my wheat,
For whiteness of the bread doth look like common *cheat*."

> Drayton, " Polyolbion," xvi., p. 250.

xv. p. 147, Epig. 2, line 1, evidently means, "yet *thou could'st* not command content." The ellipsis occurs also in Walpole's printed copy. In line 2 of the third stanza, p. 148, " swad " is a countryman; a rude clown.

xvi.—xix. pp. 149—160. *Sir Edward Dyer.* Dyer is another member of the Elizabethan court-circle whose poetry was so early lost in the mass of unappropriated and fugitive verses, that though Puttenham had praised him in 1589 as " for elegy most sweet, solemn, and of high conceit," Edmund Bolton in the next reign said, that he had "not seen much of Sir Edward Dyer's poetry " (see other references in Park's edition of Warton, H. E. P. iii. 230). We are fortunately now in a position to give a rather more complete account of it. Mr. Collier has discovered and described two rare works by Dyer; " The Praise of Nothing," 1585, which is chiefly in prose, and " Six Idyllia of Theocritus," 1588, a metrical translation (see his " Life of Spenser," p. lxxvi. note, and his " Bibl. Cat." i. 237; ii. 24, 60). Of Dyer's minor poetry, I have here printed four very characteristic specimens; two of which possess the special interest, that the replies and imitations annexed to them remind us that Sidney, Dyer, and Greville formed a close brotherhood of poets; as Sidney himself has recorded in a poem printed in Davison's " Poetical Rhapsody,"—"upon his meeting with his two worthy friends and fellow poets, Sir Edward Dyer and Mr. Fulke Greville." To these four, the following pieces may be added:

5. " Alas, my heart, mine eye hath wronged thee."—England's Helicon, p. 88 ; " S. E. Dyer."

6. " Amaryllis was full fair."—MS. Rawl. Poet. 85, fol. 98, *verso*, " E. Dier."   Also in MS. Tann. 306, p. 174.

7. " Among the woes of those unhappy wights." —A long elegy on Sidney, containing from fifty-four to sixty-one stanzas of six lines each ; printed from Breton, but without any author's name, in Bishop Butler's " Sidneiana," pp. 41—53; and identified as Dyer's in Chetham MS. 8012, pp. 143—153, where the title is " An epitaph composed by Sir Edward Dyer of Sir Philip Sidney."   As Breton's in MS. Rawl. Poet. 85, fol. 23.

8. " As rare to hear as seldom to be seen."— MS. Rawl. Poet. 85, fol. 7, *verso*. " M. Dier."

9. " Divide my times and race my wretched hours."—MS. Rawl. Poet. 85, fol. 37 ; " M. Dier."

10. " If pleasures be in painfulness."—P. of D. D. p. 20; " M. D." Dyer's claim is admitted by Ritson and Dyce.

11. " I would it were not as it is."—MS. Rawl. Poet. 85, fol. 6. " M. Dier."

Another piece beginning " O more than most fair, full of the living fire," which is signed " M. Dier " in MS. Rawl. Poet. 85, fol. 7, *verso*, is really one of Spenser's Sonnets ; No. VIII., vol. v., p. 119, Collier. A poem of Lord Brooke's begins in the same way, " Works," 1633, p. 162, but the pieces are different. It is only another instance of the poetical intercourse between these writers.

We may also add several quotations in Putten-ham's " Art of Poesy," 1589, pp. 141, 176, 198. The following pieces have been ascribed to Dyer, but appear to belong properly to Thomas Lodge; and I think the list could be extended:

1. "Alas, how wander I amidst these woods."—E. H., p. 183; "S. E. D." But it is in Lodge's "Rosalind," p. 120, reprint.

2. "Like desert woods with darksome shades obscured."—E. H., p. 112; "S. E. D." but repeated on p. 224, with the signature *Ignoto*. Hence claimed for Sir W. Raleigh by Brydges and the Oxford editors. A copy occurs in the "Phœnix Nest," 1593, p. 59, with the signature, "T. L. Gent."

3. "My Phyllis hath the morning sun."—E. H. p. 53; "S. E. D." Accepted by Ellis. But see Collier, "Bibl. Cat." i. 72, 467.

4. "When the dog," &c.—E. H., p. 154; "S. E. D." But it is in Lodge's "Rosalind," p. 120.

Mr. Collier also conjectures that the poem, "A shepherd poor, Eubulus called he was," which is commonly ascribed to Francis Davison, may have been really written by Sir E. Dyer; "Bibl. Cat." i. 188; and Malone proposed, as I have noted before (p. 215), to ascribe to him the elegy on Sidney, beginning, "Silence augmenteth grief, writing increaseth rage."

XVI. p. 149. I have given a full account of the various editions and imitations of this favourite poem in my former volume, p. lxv. note. The authority of this one MS. is considerable, because of the number of Dyer's pieces which it has preserved; and popular as the poem was, I am not aware that there is any other claimant for it.

XVII. p. 151. All the printed copies, old and new, so far as I have seen them, and also the Rawlinson MS., give in the third line the unintelligible reading, "Fond of *delight*." For the true reading,

" Fond of *the light*," we are indebted to the Har-
leian MS. In line 6, "wood"= mad. Herrick has
a short poem on the same conceit:

> " I played with love, as with the fire
> The wanton satyr did," &c.

> " That satyr he but burnt his lips,
> But mine's the greater smart," &c.
> " Poems," p. 217, ed. Hazlitt.

XVIII. p. 153. In line 3, both MSS. read " the
matter *of mishap*," which destroys the rhyme.
There are, however, many variations between
them.

XIX. p. 154. This poem must have been highly
esteemed to have obtained the compliment of
adaptation and imitation from Robert Southwell
and Lord Brooke; and yet I am not aware that it
has ever been printed before, except very imper-
fectly among the " Poems of Pembroke and Rud-
yard," and some extracts by Malone. The MS.
copies differ exceedingly, both in various readings
and in omissions. I have made out the best text
that I could, from a careful comparison of all the
materials. It is the same piece which Wood
erroneously called " A Description of Friendship "
(A. O. i. 741); a title which he took by mistake
from another poem in the Ashmole MS.

Page 156, line 16. " I read the hyacint" (so
spelt for the rhyme); *i. e.* read the fancied letters
on its leaves:—"on which are writ the *letters* of
our woe" (Beaumont). See Ovid, Metam. x. 215.
Some copies have "*reap* the hyacinth."

Page 159, line 5. " Heben;" so often Spenser,
for ebony; "His spear of *heben* wood."—" F. Q."
I. vii. st. 37.

Page 168, line 27. I have substituted " wrath"

for " worth ;" and have corrected two or three other errors of the press in different parts of the poem.

Page 171, line 9. " The ship of Greece " is clearly the famous ship in which Theseus returned after slaying the Minotaur. The Athenians professed to preserve it till the days of Demetrius Phale-reus, the rotten timbers being carefully removed and renewed from time to time, so that it became a favourite question whether a ship of which every plank had been often changed could still be called the same (Plutarch, *Thes.* p. 10, ed. 1620). This passage, in which Lord Brooke compares the changes of his mistress to that ship of Greece and to the ever-flowing stream—the same, yet not the same—perpetually altering, yet bearing continuously " their antique name,"—is an excellent specimen of the subtle conceptions which he loved to elaborate in his poetry. But the whole poem is raised to a level of thought curiously different from that of the two pieces by Dyer and Southwell with which it is connected.

xxII. p. 173. I have inserted this pretty poem from the works of Lodge, because his verses have been so much mixed up with those of Dyer. Lodge was first an Oxford student; then a voyager; next a lawyer; finally a physician ; and died of the plague in 1625. He had also a literary connection with the dramatist Robert Greene, who frequently uses the same imagery; *e. g.* in his "Never too late," 1590 :—" Then shall heaven cease to have stars, the earth trees, the world elements, and every-thing reversed shall fall to their former chaos" (Dyce, " Life of Greene," p. ix.). And in " Alphon-sus, King of Arragon " (Dyce, ii. 18) :

" For first shall heaven want stars, and foaming seas
Want watery drops, before I'll traitor be
Unto Alphonsus, whom I honour so."

XXIII. p. 174. Observe the use of adjectives for substantives ; page 175, line 14, "bright" for brightness ; line 17, " pure" for purity.

XXIV.—VI. *Robert, Earl of Essex.* To these three poems, by Elizabeth's brilliant but ill-starred favourite, the following may be added :

4. " Change thy mind, since she doth change." Douland's " Musical Banquet," &c., 1610, Cantus II., by "the Right Hon. Robert Earl of Essex, Earl Marshal of England." Anonymously in " Wit's Interpreter," 1671, p. 128 ; and MS. Rawl. Poet. 85, fol. 126.

5. " There [It] was a time when silly bees could speak."—Printed from a Sloane MS. by Park, Walpole's " R. and N. A.," ii. 113. Another MS. is quoted by Mr. Collier, " Bibl. Cat." ii. 189. The first three stanzas were printed in a music-book of Dowland's ; Percy Soc. vol. xiii. p. 72. Other copies occur in Harl. MS. 6910, fol. 167 ; in MS. Ashm. 767, fol. 1, and 781, p. 132 ; and in MS. Tann. 306, p. 249.

6. " Muses no more, but Mazes be your name." —Harl. MS. 6910, fol. 151, as by " Comes Essex." Thence printed in " Exc. Tudor." vol. i. p. 33. .

7. " To plead my faith where faith hath no reward."—Douland, 1610, as above ; Cantus VI.

Another poem is found in MS. Ashm. 767, fol. 64, entitled " Essex's last Voyage to the Haven of Happiness," beginning, " Welcome, sweet death, the kindest friend I have." But this piece seems to be merely an elegy on his demise ; after the manner of " The Lieutenant's Legend," or " The

despairing Complaint of wretched Raleigh." Sir
Henry Wotton says that "to evaporate his
thoughts in a Sonnet" was Essex's "common
way;" and from one of these he quotes the couplet
(" Rel. Wotton." p. 165, ed. 1685):

" And if thou should'st by her be now forsaken,
She made thy heart too strong for to be shaken."

The history of " his darling piece of love and self-
love " (ib. p. 174), appears to have been made out
sufficiently by Mr. Spedding; "Life of Bacon,"
vol. i. pp. 374-391. Mr. Hallam passes a very high
eulogium on his prose; "Literature of Europe,"
vol. iii. p. 145, ed. 1843. I am not aware that his
supposed translation of one of Ovid's Epistles has
been found; Warton, H. E. P., iii. 340-1.

XXVII.—VIII. pp. 178-181. *A. W.* It is very re-
markable that no clue has been discovered to the
owner of these initials, the author of a large portion
of the best poems in Davison's "Poetical Rhap-
sody." At one time Brydges had proposed to give
Raleigh the credit of the entire series, which had up
to that time been anonymous; but the intention
was defeated by the production of a list, which Sir
H. Nicolas pronounces to be in the handwriting of
Francis Davison himself, entitled, " Catalogue of
all the poems in rhyme or measured verse by
A. W." (Harl. MS. 280, fol. 102), and including all
the poems in question. It is impossible to with-
hold our sympathy for Brydges' disappointment.
The guess was a good one. The poems would
have done Raleigh no dishonour. They present
many marks of strong resemblance to his authen-
ticated poems; and the longer piece which I have
here inserted would have commended itself to
every one as a natural and appropriate statement

of Raleigh's gradual change of style, and progress towards maturity of thought.

XXXI. p. 183. These specimens of elegies ou the premature death of Henry, Prince of Wales, are taken from one of the reprints in Mr. Laing's "Fugitive Scottish Poetry of the XVIIth century," 1825. The editor remarks, p. vi., that the signature *Ignoto* is here "supposed to designate Sir Walter Raleigh." Raleigh's feelings on the death of a prince, in whose grave his hopes were buried, are expressed with touching brevity in the last sentence of his "History of the World;" "whereas this book, by the title it hath, calls itself the first part of the general History of the World, implying a second and third volume, which I also intended and have hewn out ; besides many other discouragements persuading my silence, it hath pleased God to take that glorious prince out of the world, to whom they were directed ; whose unspeakable and never enough lamented loss hath taught me to say with Job (xxx. 31), *versa est in luctum cithara mea, et organum meum in vocem flentium.*"

XXXIII.—v. pp. 187-191. *George Sandys.* This writer, whose name carries us back (through his brother Edwin) to the days of Richard Hooker, and whose versification received the praises of both Dryden and Pope, occupied several offices of trust under the crown, and addressed his royal patrons in several dedications, both in verse and prose. The word "god-like," page 187, line 14, may be understood simply in the official sense, of the "divinity" that "doth hedge a king;" as in King James's Sonnet, above, No. xxix., "God gives not kings the style of gods in vain ;" or as Lord Bacon,

Essay XIX., " All precepts concerning kings are in
effect comprehended in those two remembrances :
Memento quod es homo; and *Memento quod es Deus,*
or *vice Dei;* the one bridleth their power, and the
other their will."

XXXIV. p. 188. This striking commemoration
of his perils can be partially illustrated from his
" Travels," on at least the Eastern side.   For the
Simoans, see pp. 15, 28; he had gone on board
"a bark Armado of Simo, a little island hard
by the Rhodes," the sailors of which indulged in
a drunken disturbance which is vividly described.
For Arabian thieves, see pp. 138-9; for the Emir
of Sidon, pp. 210-2; though this story seems to be
but partly told.   It can scarcely be necessary to
refer for the letters of Bellerophon to Homer,
Iliad, VI. 168.

XXXV. p. 191. This undoubtedly genuine poem
of Sandys has found its way into the Works of
Drummond of Hawthornden, 1711; Poems, p. 45;
not the only instance of misappropriation in that
collection.

XXXVI. p. 192. It is now agreed on all hands
that this is only " a broad-sheet ballad " on the
death of Strafford; though the unknown writer
has for once risen far above the level of his class.
" The Lieutenant's Legend," which is, doubtless,
just as little genuine, is reprinted in Park's Wal-
pole, " R. and N. A.," vol. ii. pp. 335-9.   It begins :

> " Eye me, ye mounting cedars; once was I,
>   As you are, great; rich in the estimate
> Of prince and people; no malignant eye
>   Reflected on me; so secure my state," &c.

XXXVII. p. 195. The word " earthly" in line 2

is a suggestion of the Archbishop of Dublin's, to complete the imperfect metre.

XXXVIII. p. 200. In line 5, "sophy" is changed in most modern editions to *sophist*. The word, which occurs in Shakespeare, &c., as a Persian title, is used by Giles Fletcher for the Magians :

> " To see their king the kingly *Sophies* come."
> "Christ's Victory," 1610, st. lxxxii, p. 24.

Page 200, line 19. The reference is to the story how Jason of Pheræ *medicinam invenit ex hoste*, when the dagger of an assassin saved his life by opening an imposthume which his physicians had given over as incurable: Pliny, H. N. vii. 51; Cicero, De Nat. D. iii. 28; Valerius Maximus, I. viii. Externa, § 6.

Page 201, stanza ix. This stanza is rejected by Lady Theresa Lewis, as at variance with the drift and purport of the poem; "Clarendon Gallery," vol. ii. p. 183, note. But it is found in the original 4to., and in Lloyd. The copies of the poem differ widely, both in arrangement and in readings.

XXXIX—XLI., pp. 203-207. *Marquis of Montrose.* The fragments of verse ascribed by Watson and others to Montrose have been collected with great care by Mr. Mark Napier. It is sufficient therefore to refer to his work for details on the following list, which is given in continuation of the six pieces here printed : —

7. "As Macedo his Homer, I'll thee still." Six lines on Lucan ; Napier, p. 60.

8. "Burst out, my soul, in main of tears." Supposed to have been written on the death of Charles I.; *ib.* Appendix, p. xlii.

9. "Here lies a dog whose quality did plead." From Balfour's MSS., *ib.* p. 377.

10. " There's nothing in this world can prove."
Ib. Appendix, p. xli.

11. " When Heaven's great Jove had made the
world's round frame." *Ib.* Appendix, p. xl.

Another fragment which Mr. Napier has retain-
ed from Watson, Appendix, p. xl., and p. 464, has
been printed above, p. 232, from the " Aberdeen
Song Book," 1682, where it forms the last verse
of a continuation of Sir H. Wotton's poem on
the Queen of Bohemia. The second part of the
Ballad No. xxxix. consists of thirteen additional
stanzas ; Napier, Appendix, p. xxxv. It begins :

" My dear and only love, take heed—"

But Mr. Chappell gives reasons for supposing
that this other piece dates from the reign of James
I., and Montrose was only born in 1612.

Page 204, line 13. This is Mr. Napier's text ;
but most copies retain the Scottish pronunciation,
" Or *committees* if thou erect." In the last stanza,
also, I follow Mr. Napier ; and annex here the
better-known reading given by Sir W. Scott,
" Legend of Montrose," ch. xv. :

" But if no faithless action stain
Thy true and constant word,
I'll make thee famous by my pen,
And glorious by my sword :
I'll serve thee in such noble ways
As ne'er were known before ;
I'll deck and crown thy head with bays,
And love thee more and more."

Page 206, line 5. " Paragon " is used for *equal,
parallel,* or *rival.* Shakespeare employs it in the
same sense as a verb :

" If thou with Cæsar *paragon* again
My man of men."
" Antony and Cleopatra," i. 5.

I.

INDEX OF FIRST LINES.

II.

INDEX OF AUTHORS.

BACON, FRANCIS, LORD.   Part II. Nos. xxii. xxiii.
BROOKE, FULKE GREVILLE, LORD.   Part III. No. xxi.
BROOKE, SAMUEL, D.D.   Part II. No. xix.
CHARLES I., KING.   Part III. No. xxxvii.
DYER, SIR EDWARD.   Part III. Nos. xvi. xvii. xviii. xix.;
    with list of his other Poems among the Notes, p. 243.
ELIZABETH, QUEEN.   Part III. No. viii.
ESSEX, ROBERT, EARL OF.   Part III. Nos. xxiv. xxv.
    xxvi.; with list of his other Poems among the Notes,
    p. 248.
GORGES, SIR ARTHUR.   Part III. No. xxx.   See also p.
    229.
HARYNGTON, JOHN.   Part III. Nos. vi. (doubtful) vii.
HEYWOOD, JOHN.   Part III. No. ii. (very doubtful.)
HEYWOOD, THOMAS.   Part I. No. xxvii. (very doubtful.)
HOSKINS, JOHN.   Part II. Nos. ii. (in part), xxv.
HUNNIS, WILLIAM.   Part I. No. xxv. (doubtful.)   Part III.
    No. iv. (doubtful.)
JAMES I., KING.   Part III. No. xxix.
JONSON, BEN.   Part II. No. xi. (an erroneous claim.)
    Part III. No. xxxii.
L'ESTRANGE, SIR ROGER. . Part III. No. xxxviii.
LODGE, THOMAS.   Part III. No. xxii.
M., F.   Part III. No. xv. 3.
MARLOWE, CHRISTOPHER.   Part I. No. vi. 1.

MONTROSE, JAMES, MARQUIS OF.   Part. III. Nos. xxxix.
    xl. xli.; with list of his other Poems among the Notes,
    p. 252.
OXFORD, EDWARD, EARL OF.   Part III. Nos. xi. xii. xiii.
    xiv. xv. 1; with list of his other Poems among the
    Notes, p. 241.
PEMBROKE, MARY, COUNTESS OF.   Part III. No. x.
RALEIGH, SIR WALTER.   All Part I., except No. vi. 1.
    But Nos. xxv. xxvi. xxvii. xxviii. xxix. and xxx. are
    doubtful.   The following also have been assigned to
    him, though on insufficient evidence: Part II. Nos
    iv. xvi. xvii. xviii. xx. 1. xxi. xxiv. 1.   Part III. Nos.
    xxiii. xxviii.   See also Appendix to the Introduction, B.
ROCHFORD, VISCOUNT.   Part III. No. i. (doubtful.)
S., E.   Part I. No. xxv. (doubtful.)
SANDYS, GEORGE.   Part III. Nos. xxxiii. xxxiv. xxxv.
SIDNEY, SIR PHILIP.   Part III. Nos. ix. xv. 2, xvii. 2.
SOUTHWELL, ROBERT.   Part III. No. xx.
TYCHBOURNE, CHIDIOCK.   Part II. No. xx. 1.
UNCERTAIN OR UNKNOWN (besides other poems in this list
    marked "doubtful.") Part II. Nos. xvi. xvii. xviii. xx.
    2, xxi. xxiv. Part III. Nos. ii. xv. 4, xxiii. xxxi. xxxvi.
VAUX, THOMAS, LORD.   Part III.   Nos. iii. iv. (doubtful),
    v. vi. (doubtful); with list of his Poems among the
    Notes, p. 238.
W., A.   Part III. Nos. xxvii. xxviii.
WOTTON, SIR HENRY.   Part II. Nos. i. ii. (in part), iii.
    iv. v. vi. vii. viii. ix. x. xi. xii. xiii. xiv. xv. and
    perhaps also Nos. xvi. and xvii.
WYATT, SIR THOMAS.   Part III. No. i. (doubtful.)

CHISWICK PRESS:—PRINTED BY WHITTINGHAM AND WILKINS,
TOOKS COURT, CHANCERY LANE.

www.ingramcontent.com/pod-product-compliance
Lightning Source LLC
Chambersburg PA
CBHW021039030726

47496CB00006B/1604